Frontispiece. Above: The L'A.C.F. Grand Prix 1912, a coloured lithograph by Gamy.
Below: Another lithograph of the L'A.C.F. Grand Prix, this time the 1913 event, also by Gamy. Both vehicles featured are Peugeots.

The Price Guide
and
Identification
of
AUTOMOBILIA

Gordon Gardiner
and
Alistair Morris

Antique Collectors' Club

Published for the Antique Collectors' Club
by the Antique Collectors' Club Ltd.

Gardiner, Gordon
    The price guide and identification of automobilia
    1. Automobiles — Equipment and supplies
    — Collectors and collecting
    I. Title   II. Morris, Alistair
    629.2'222   TL159

Printed in England by Baron Publishing, Woodbridge, Suffolk

Antique Collectors' Club

The Antique Collectors' Club was formed in 1966 and now has a five figure membership spread throughout the world. It publishes the only independently run monthly antiques magazine *Antique Collecting* which caters for those collectors who are interested in widening their knowledge of antiques, both by greater awareness of quality and by discussion of the factors which influence the price that is likely to be asked. The Antique Collectors' Club pioneered the provision of information on prices for collectors and the magazine still leads in the provision of detailed articles on a variety of subjects.

It was in response to the enormous demand for information on "what to pay" that the price guide series was introduced in 1968 with the first edition of *The Price Guide to Antique Furniture* (completely revised, 1978), a book which broke new ground by illustrating the more common types of antique furniture, the sort that collectors could buy in shops and at auctions rather than the rare museum pieces which had previously been used (and still to a large extent are used) to make up the limited amount of illustrations in books published by commercial publishers. Many other price guides have followed, all copiously illustrated, and greatly appreciated by collectors for the valuable information they contain, quite apart from prices. The Antique Collectors' Club also publishes other books on antiques, including horology and art reference works, and a full book list is available.

Club membership, which is open to all collectors, costs £9.95 per annum. Members receive free of charge *Antique Collecting,* the Club's magazine (published every month except August), which contains well-illustrated articles dealing with the practical aspects of collecting not normally dealt with by magazines. Prices, features of value, investment potential, fakes and forgeries are all given prominence in the magazine.

Among other facilities available to members are private buying and selling facilities, the longest list of "For Sales" of any antiques magazine, an annual ceramics conference and the opportunity to meet other collectors at their local antique collectors' clubs. There are nearly eighty in Britain and so far a dozen overseas. Members may also buy the Club's publications at special pre-publication prices.

As its motto implies, the Club is an amateur organisation designed to help collectors to get the most out of their hobby: it is informal and friendly and gives enormous enjoyment to all concerned.

For Collectors — By Collectors — About Collecting

The Antique Collectors' Club, 5 Church Street, Woodbridge, Suffolk

Price Revision List

Published annually in November
(the first list will be published in 1983)

The usefulness of a book containing prices rapidly diminishes as market values change.

In order to keep the prices in this book updated, a price revision list will be issued in November each year. This will record the major price changes in the values of the items covered under the various headings in the book.

To ensure you receive the price revision list, complete the pro forma invoice inserted in this book and send it to the address below:

**ANTIQUE COLLECTORS' CLUB
5 CHURCH STREET, WOODBRIDGE, SUFFOLK**

Contents

Colour Plates

continued

continued

Acknowledgements

Particular thanks to Peter Moore of Motor Book Postal Auctions for general interest and assistance, and to Peter W. Card for his interest and advice with regard to the lamp section.

Hazel Gardiner	W. Leslie Weller
Eric Campion	Bob Dawes
Joe Lyndhurst	Justine Michaels
Derek Kingsbury	Jenni Clarke
John Bray	Gordon Lang
Roy Butler	Dendy Easton
Ian Dean	Peter Pawson
Warren Butcher	Jeremy Rye
Dennis Rendell	Stephen Adams
Bobbie Morris	Hilary Kay
Neil Blackstone	Alison Fox
Cherry Lewis	Kerry Taylor
Alison Blyth	Alan Bennet
Primrose Elliott	D.R. Blair
Diana McMillan	J.N. Carstairs
	Sarah Cousins

Photographic Credits

Sotheby's Pulborough	Sotheby's Belgravia
Motor Book Postal Auctions	Dawes & Billings
Chalk Pits Museum, Amberley	Wallis & Wallis
Warnham War Museum	Adrian Weller
A.G. Blackstone	John Lay
J.I. Elliott	Lester Hall

In addition, our thanks to the following for their kind permission to reproduce illustrations from original catalogues:

Messrs. Brown Bros.
Quinton Hazell Ltd.
The Scottish Heritage Trust Ltd.

Foreword

The armchair traveller would presumably prefer actually to go on a journey than just read about it, or can it be assumed that the growth in the collecting of items associated with the motor car is due to the fact that the real thing is too rich for the blood of the average enthusiast?

Certainly a contributory factor, but not more than that.

The real truth of the matter is that the material has enormous appeal in its own right. Much talent went into producing these items, and none of us needs any excuse to wish to own them.

Throughout its history, the selling of the motor car and its components has been the most tremendous struggle. Men worked in the teeth of intense competition, recessions and just plain fashion. Skilled engineers, artists in metal-work and artists of art and photography, cunning advertising men and stylists and an army of people fought this battle. No hobbyists here, necessity was the mother of their invention. Their livings, sometimes fragile, often frugal, dictated that their artistry be their best.

Their talents have not been entirely ignored in the past. Breakers and owners always kept the mascots and the clocks and sometimes the badges. Sometimes instruments and horns for a while anyway.

Paperwork suffered of course. Showrooms threw out last year's catalogues without a thought. I always have felt that the schoolboys, those pests of the motor shows, were the principal reason why those catalogues that have survived, did so. (The enemy that was Mother, tidying the bedroom, had to be another hurdle...)

Recently I spoke to a man who was intrigued enough to collect Mr. Bibendum in his many forms — that beloved little fellow, and a device that must have contributed so greatly to Michelin sales. As much as any advertising creation ever did for any firm. This collector was not interested in any other motoring material.

Of such is the broad fabric of the automobilia collectors' world. Whether the motive is intrigue, nostalgia, association (love of a marque, art, gain or just plain acquisitiveness, these people all have something in common. They need knowledge. The owners of the cars need knowledge too. What P100 is right for what car? At £150 plus, they need to be right. Such enthusiasts, and the many thousands of motor car lovers all over the world, will find this work both useful and fascinating. I already have.

Peter Moore
Pulborough
September 1982

Introduction

Although there has always been considerable interest in the automobile, there can be no doubt that the collection of vintage and veteran vehicles requires considerable financial, storage and operational involvement. However, next to this world exists an equally interesting and rewarding collecting area which in many of its facets is comparatively new, and can still be enjoyed by those with a modest budget.

To emphasise the development of this field, it is interesting to trace the growth of the now famous Beaulieu 'Autojumble' which started as a small event in 1967 with approximately seventy stallholders, many of whom were disposing of unwanted 'spares' and which this year (1982) attracted nearly 1,400 stallholders and over 30,000 people from all over the world. As may be seen from this book, not only established items, such as mascots and lamps, but also innumerable accessories and 'paraphernalia' may be sought after. In recent years, a network of local autojumbles has appeared to satisfy regional interests, also many dealers operate full time shops and even the large auction houses hold periodic specialist sales. For those keen to improve their knowledge, several good motor museums have been established and many good motor magazines exist which can include articles and advertisements relating to automobilia.

As with all forms of collecting, it is better to form a collection which pleases rather than attempt to acquire an accumulation of unrelated items in poor condition. Whereas many areas of automobilia have proved a good investment, condition would appear to be the prime factor, as it is with many other collecting fields. However, in order to give a balance to this book, items in various grades of condition will be encountered and priced accordingly.

This book is intended as a visual reference, with identification and general interest comments, and some old catalogue illustrations, as well as a price guide for use by collector and dealer alike. The period covered ranges from circa 1900 to 1950. The vast majority of photographs have been specially taken for this work and in some instances more than one view has been used to emphasise a point. Colour illustrations have been incorporated to bring back to life the aesthetic charm of many of these items.

The authors are aware that when assessing values of automobilia (as indeed with many other types of antiques and collectable items) there may be considerable variations from area to area, and that both dealer and auction prices are also subject to fluctuating conditions. In researching prices for this book, the authors have endeavoured to take these facts into account and from necessity an average price has had to be assessed. Careful attention must be given to condition; remember many of these items were fitted to the exterior of vehicles and were subjected to the elements, other items may have been produced as promotional material which could have been easily damaged and discarded — all mint examples are therefore likely to be scarce.

Lamps

Subject to availability of space, one of the most visually attractive motoring items must be lamps.

Early head lamps of polished brass or nickel plated finish (or a combination of finishes to include japanned, oxidised and enamelled black) were usually acetylene, as this produced a good beam, and were either of self-contained type or reservoir operated. Side and tail lamps were usually oil and were less expensive to produce. All these lamps were readily detachable from the vehicle, a fact that has probably contributed to their survival, since lamps were removed and retained when the vehicle was scrapped.

Although electric lamps were available, it was not until after World War I that they saw general use and became fixtures on the vehicles requiring less maintenance. Various bulb locations and reflector systems were used. Major quality producers were Zeiss, Marchal, Grebel and the most expensive of the Lucas range, notably P.100s.

Post-war, the head lamp retracted into the bodywork.

1. A pair of oil side lamps, known as Opera lamps from the days when such lamps were used as parking lights while the vehicle owner attended the Opera or theatre. Small faceted ruby lenses to rear.
£30 — £50 each
£80 — £120 pair

2. Unusual, this pair of early oil side lamps is painted black with polished brass rims and oil reservoirs. Lens diameter 4½ins.:11.5cm, height 13½ins.:34cm. Circa 1908-12.
£150 — £200

3. A good quality large size side lamp, oil burning, brass frame with bevelled glasses. Circa 1910. Below, the reverse side showing faceted ruby lens for rear and mounting socket.

£35 — £50
more than double for a pair

4. From a 1911 catalogue, Lucas products including: top, electric side lamps of the 'Opera Light' form, forward facing lens clear, near lens ruby red, and side lens 'Bristol' blue with star cut decoration. Underneath are oil powered side and tail lamps, note lamp on right showing red rear facing lens with smaller clear (white) lens to illuminate number plate.

6. A brass oil side lamp by Powell and Hanmer, with bevelled glass lens, fixed carrying handle (fore and aft type) and mounting bracket. 11ins.:28cm high. Circa 1910.

£40 — £60

5. Fine and unusual, a Rolls brass oil tail lamp having a 4ins.:10cm diameter bull's-eye ruby lens and folding carrying handle with clip (handle folded in top picture). A superior product. Possibly Lucas for Charles Rolls, scarce. Circa 1903-05.

£100 — £130

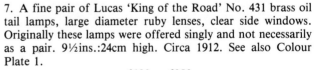

7. A fine pair of Lucas 'King of the Road' No. 431 brass oil tail lamps, large diameter ruby lenses, clear side windows. Originally these lamps were offered singly and not necessarily as a pair. 9½ins.:24cm high. Circa 1912. See also Colour Plate 1.

£180 — £250

8. From the Lucas range, 'King of the Road' brass oil tail lamps, No. 631. Produced c.1907-31. On this model the large diameter lens is clear glass for number plate illumination. Also smaller ruby lens. Although polished brass, this model was originally catalogued as ebony black with plated parts and priced at £1. 15s. in 1911. The lamp on the right shows mounting bracket and wick cover, 10ins.:25.5cm high. The lamps illustrated are circa 1925.

£50 — £80 each

9. A pair of Lucas 'King of the Road' No. 742 side lamps, brass with steel oil reservoirs, convex lenses 4¾ins.:12cm diameter. Fixed carrying handles. 14¼ins.:36cm high. Note double socket, commercial type. Long production life, 1907-31.

£120 — £180

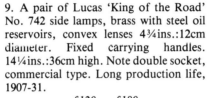

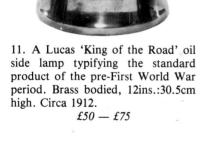

11. A Lucas 'King of the Road' oil side lamp typifying the standard product of the pre-First World War period. Brass bodied, 12ins.:30.5cm high. Circa 1912.

£50 — £75

10. A Lucas 'King of the Road' No. 742 side lamp — originally black japanned, now polished brass. This lamp was produced for use with large vehicles. Circa 1911. 13¼ins.:34cm high. Note rim damage, original price for pair £4. 8s. 0d. (£4.40).

£12 — £18 due to condition

12. Also produced by Lucas, this 'King's Own' oil side lamp of brass. This model was a new pattern from 1914 to c.1931; in 1914 this type, part of a 'King's Own' set, included a generator and head lamps. Used singularly on light cars and cycle cars. 8¼ins.:21cm high.

£12 — £20 rather poor condition

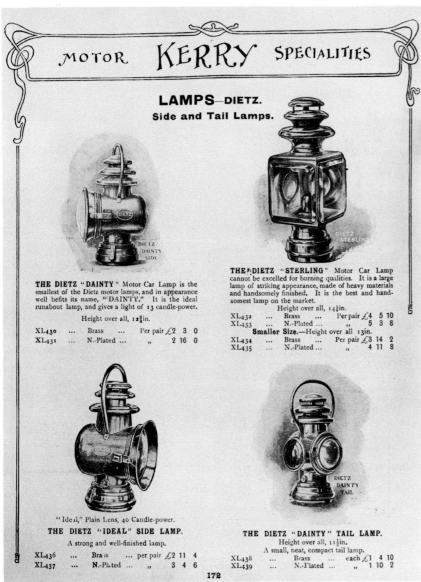

MOTOR **KERRY** SPECIALITIES

LAMPS—DIETZ.
Side and Tail Lamps.

THE DIETZ "DAINTY" Motor Car Lamp is the smallest of the Dietz motor lamps, and in appearance well befits its name, "DAINTY." It is the ideal runabout lamp, and gives a light of 13 candle-power.

Height over all, 12¾in.

XL430	...	Brass	... Per pair £2	3 0
XL431	...	N.-Plated	... ,, 2	16 0

THE DIETZ "STERLING" Motor Car Lamp cannot be excelled for burning qualities. It is a large lamp of striking appearance, made of heavy materials and handsomely finished. It is the best and handsomest lamp on the market.

Height over all, 14½in.

XL432	...	Brass	Per pair £4	5 10
XL433	...	N.-Plated ...	,,	5 3 8

Smaller Size.—Height over all 13in.

XL434	...	Brass	Per pair £3	14 2
XL435	...	N.-Plated ...	,, 4	11 8

"Ideal," Plain Lens, 40 Candle-power.
THE DIETZ "IDEAL" SIDE LAMP.
A strong and well-finished lamp.

XL436	...	Brass	... per pair £2	11 4
XL437	...	N.-Plated ...	,,	3 4 6

THE DIETZ "DAINTY" TAIL LAMP.
Height over all, 11½in.
A small, neat, compact tail lamp.

XL438	...	Brass	... each £1	4 10
XL439	...	N.-Plated ...	,, 1	10 2

172

13. These American produced lamps from 'Dietz' illustrate a standard range. Note the early model 'T' Ford normally carried Dietz lamps.

Top right: 14. A Dietz 'Eureka' oil tail lamp with ruby lens, folding carrying handle and side mounted bracket. Of the type used on Model 'T' Fords. 7ins.:18cm high. Circa 1914.

£40 — £50

Right: 15. A slightly distressed and repaired Lucas oil tail lamp, part steel, part brass construction, commercial vehicle type. Note catch at base, an early feature. Circa 1910-1920.

£25 — £40

MOTOR KERRY SPECIALITIES

LAMPS—continued.
DEPENDENCE.

SPECIFICATION.

Large Size.
Height, 8½in. Ruby Glass, 4in. diameter.
Side Glasses, 4in × 2½in.

Small Size.
Height, 7½in. Ruby Glass, 3½in. diameter.
Side Glasses, 3½ × 2in.

FINISH—Large Size.

XL336	Enamelled, with Brass Mounting	501	22/6
XL337	„ Plated „	502	26/4
XL338	All Brass	503	37/6
XL339	All Nickelled	504	45/0

The Popular SMALL SIZE.

XL340	Enamelled, with Brass Mounting	506	18/10
XL341	„ Plated „	507	22/6
XL342	All Brass	508	31/6
XL343	All Nickelled	509	37/6

Smallest Size.—Suitable for Motor Cabs, Tricars, etc.
Height, 6in. Bail adds 2in. Ruby Glass, 3in. diameter.
Side Glasses, 3in. × 1½in.

XL344	Finish Enamelled, with Brass Mounts	540	16/0
XL345	„ „ Plated „	573	18/10
XL346	Oil Wells and Burners for the Small and Tricar lamps, 5/0 each.		
XL347	„ „ for large size, Nos. 501-504		5/6 „

1911 Type fitted with New Improved Electric Adapter. Rear Lamp FOR OIL AND ELECTRIC

LARGE SIZE.

XL349	All Brass, complete as illustrated...	521 each	46/6
XL350	Ditto N.P.	522 „	54/0
XL351	Enamelled with Brass Mounts „	519 „	31/6
XL352	„ N.P. „ „	520 „	35/0

The Popular SMALL SIZE.

XL353	All Brass...	525 each	40/6
XL354	Ditto N.P.	526 „	46/6
XL355	Enamelled with Brass Mounts	523 „	28/0
XL356	„ N.P.	524 „	31/6

INTERCHANGEABLE ELECTRIC ADAPTER.

XL357 Complete with 2 yards
35/40 Vulcanized Flexible Wire
Holder, and 4 volt lamp, 7/6 each.

GARAGE SAFETY WALL LAMP.
(REGISTERED.)

Type No. 541. **SPECIFICATION.**
Height, 18in. Glass Front, 11×11×6in. Glass Sides, 11×3½×5½in.
Burning capacity, 15 hours.

XL348 Burns Paraffin ... Price 37/6 each.
This Lamp is expressly designed for lighting Garages and Motor Houses where electric light is not obtainable.
The danger of illuminating with ordinary paraffin or gas in the vicinity of petrol is a very serious one, and cannot be too strongly emphasized.
This Lamp has been subjected to the most exhaustive tests with perfectly satisfactory results. It has been proved an impossibility for petrol vapour to become ignited with this Lamp in use.
A most important adjunct to every Motor House.

THE DEPENDENCE TAXIMETER LAMP.
XL358 Price ... ... each 15/0
With Bracket as illustrated 1/0 each extra.

168

16. A most interesting page from a 1911 catalogue showing 'Dependence' tail lamps, electric adaptor, garage safety wall lamps and taxi meter lamp. Note swing cover to 'For Hire' display glass. Top centre illustration indicates triple function of lamp for forward, offside and number plate illumination.

17. J. & R. Oldfield Ltd. produced lamps under the trade name 'Dependence'. Shown here is a brass side lamp type No. 887, manufacturer's details on affixed plate.

£25 — £40 each
£60 — £100 pair

Colour Plate 1. Two Lucas 'King of the Road' brass oil tail lamps with ruby lenses, 11½ins.:24cm high, circa 1912. See also no. 7.

Colour Plate 2. A fine Powell & Hanmer brass acetylene head lamp, c. 1904-14. See also no. 24.

Left: 18. A Brown Bros. No. 1109 oil tail lamp finished in black with applied Brown Bros. brass retailer's plate, intended for commercial vehicles and possibly made by Oldfield. 'Twenties and 'thirties.

£15 — £25

Centre: 19. An Oldfield 'Dependence' black enamelled oil tail lamp, this time with plain ruby lens and angled side windows.

£15 — £25

Right: 20. Another 'Dependence' product — a black enamelled oil tail lamp with brass mounts, ruby bull's-eye lens and angled side windows. Mainly used on commercial vehicles. Long production span, retailing at £1. 7s. 6d. (£1.37½) in 1937.

£15 — £25

21. Note specially designed glass (8¾ins.:22cm diameter lens) for anti-dazzle to this Salsbury ('Anti Dazlo') acetylene head lamp with British patent date 1907. Brass construction, mirror reflector. Edwardian.

£70 — £100

22. One of a pair of fine Phare Ducellier brass self-contained acetylene head lamps with 7¼ins.:18.5cm diameter lens, ruby and green port and starboard side windows. French, circa 1905. 14ins.:35.5cm high.

£300 — £400 pair

29. & 31. Gt Eastern St. London.

LAMPS—continued.

POWELL AND HANMER.   ALL BRITISH.

SELF CONTAINED HEADLIGHTS.   Acetylene.   Drip System   Burning Ordinary Carbide.

Head Lamp, No. 505.
Plain Convex Front Glass.

		£ s. d.
XL65	All Brass ... ... each	4 5 0
XL66	All Plated... ... ,,	4 17 0
XL67	Enamelled with Brass Mounts ,,	4 0 0
XL68	Enamelled with Plated Mounts	0

Head Lamp, No. 505B.
With Bull's Eye Lens. Front 9" dia., fitted with 7" plate glass lens and double convex projector.

		£ s. d.
XL69	All Brass ... each	5 2 0
XL70	All Plated ... ,,	5 13 0
XL71	Enamelled with Brass Mounts ,,	4 17 0
XL72	,, ,, Plated ,,	4 17 0

Head Lamp, No. 505L.   each.
With Dioptric Lens.

		£ s. d.
XL73	All Brass ... ,,	4 14 0
XL74	All Plated ... ,,	5 4 0
XL75	Enamelled with Brass Mounts	4 9 0
XL75	Enamelled with Plated Mounts	4 9 0

SEPARATE GENERATOR LAMPS.

P. & H. Searchlight.
Diameter of Front, 8". Reflector, 6½". Bracket Centres, 7½".
This Lamp is made upon the latest principle having a powerful Mangin mirror reflector, optically ground and properly focussed. Size of front. 8".   Type 600S.

		£ s. d.
XL77	All Brass ... each	4 0 0
XL78	All Nickel-plated on Brass ... ,,	4 7 0

This Lamp has a front 10" in diameter, fitted with an 8" convex lens, inside which is a condenser lens which projects the light far ahead. It is fitted with an aluminium Reflector.

		£ s. d.
XL79	All Brass ... ... each	4 5 0
XL80	All Plated ... ... ,,	4 17 0

P. & H. Large Generator.
Fitted with enclosed condenser in place of exposed gas bag.
Complete as illustrated in Polished Oak Case.
XL81 Brass, each £4 5 0
XL82 N.-Plated ,, ,, 4 16 0

P. & H. Double Generator.
One side can be used for a spare if required. With enclosed condenser in place of gas bag.
Complete in Polished Oak Case as illustrated.
XL83 ... each £3 12 0

158

23. An illustration from East London Rubber Company's catalogue of 1911, showing: Top, three Powell & Hanmer self-contained acetylene head lamps, note finishes available. Centre, lamps employing a separate generator, to be mounted elsewhere on the vehicle and connected by rubber pipes. Below, two generators available for use with above.

24. Two views of a brass self-contained acetylene head lamp from the Powell & Hanmer range, similar to top centre catalogue illustration in no. 23. These were stirrup mounted and detachable, for ease of cleaning carbide chamber, and could be used as a lantern if required by use of carrying handle. Note light intensifying device in the form of bull's-eye magnifying glass, called a condenser lens.

Three-quarter side view shows flip-up lid which accommodates the calcium of carbide reservoir. The multi-perforated body aids cooling but had to be carefully arranged to prevent flame being extinguished by draught. 10½ins.:27cm high. See also Colour Plate 2.

£125 — £150 each
£300 — £400 pair

25. A large Lucas 'King of the Road' Duplex model self-contained acetylene head lamp mounted on twin reservoirs with impressed instructions, black painted body with polished brass rim ventilator, chimney and handle. 4ins.:10cm diameter concave mirrored reflector. Considered a break through when introduced in 1907. Made in two sizes in 1911; dropped from the catalogue by 1922. 12½ins.:32cm high. Circa 1910.

£100 — £130

26. In as found condition, this self-contained acetylene brass head lamp is waiting to be restored to its past glory and requires careful cleaning. Bevelled glass, carrying handle, etc. Maker's plate A.D.L. Duplex Lens, 8¼ins.:21cm diameter. Circa 1912.

£75 — £100

27. An Alpha B.R.C. No. 10 self-contained acetylene head lamp in polished brass with 7ins.:18cm diameter lens, claimed to be 800 candle power. Note condensing (intensifying) lens just visible. Original cost in 1911 £6. Far left, an alternative view of another Alpha B.R.C. 'Lenticulaire Parabolique' No. 10. Note replacement glass (not bevelled).

£100 — £130

28. Another large Alpha B.R.C. No. 30 self-contained acetylene head lamp in polished brass with 10¼ins.:26cm (2,500 candle power) condensing (intensifying) lens. See also condenser chamber to lower front. Price in 1911 £13.

£140 — £180

29. Note the expense of the largest nickel plated Alpha B.R.C. self-contained head light, which claimed to give 6,000 candle power! We have noted another product from the same period with catadioptric lens which produced 10,000 candle power and cost £32. 18s. 0d. (£32.90).

30. This small brass self-contained acetylene head lamp has a 6½ins.:16.5cm lens diameter, carrying handle (bail) and graduated dial to water regulator, stirrup mounted. Circa 1910.
£75 — £100

31. In distressed condition but worthy of restoration, a 'Castle' acetyloid head lamp retaining traces of nickel finish. Circa 1910. This type of lamp operated with separate generator.
£15 — £20
poor condition, but scarce

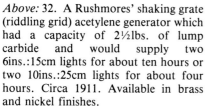

Above: 32. A Rushmores' shaking grate (riddling grid) acetylene generator which had a capacity of 2½lbs. of lump carbide and would supply two 6ins.:15cm lights for about ten hours or two 10ins.:25cm lights for about four hours. Circa 1911. Available in brass and nickel finishes.

£80 — £100

Above right: 33. Two Lucas 'King of the Road' brass self-contained acetylene motor head lamps, with carrying handles (bails). Manufacturer's plates evident to front, glass diameter 5¼ins.:13.5cm, 12¼ins.:31cm long, 10¾ins.:27cm high. Circa 1905; model dropped from catalogue by 1910.

£250 — £400 pair

34. 'King of the Road' Duplex head light by Lucas, somewhat similar to No. 25. Large size model would burn for four and a half hours, enabling a reasonably long journey to be completed without recharging. However, the model would have been an expensive purchase in 1911. Also shown are further lamps from the range, including the new product for the year, the 'Kinglite'.

MOTOR **KERRY** SPECIALITIES

LAMPS continued.—"LUCAS."

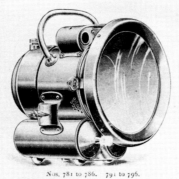

"KING OF THE ROAD" DUPLEX HEAD-LIGHT.

FITTED WITH MANGIN LENS MIRROR.

The addition of the Mangin Lens Mirror and Parabolic Reflector makes its illuminating power equal to that of the powerful Projectors.

The light falls on the road exactly where it is required, giving a sufficiently wide beam of highly penetrative light, with a broader light of less intensity covering the road, and clearly indicating the borders or hedges.

Nos. 781 to 786. 791 to 796.

Large Size.

Fits Standard Brackets, 7¼ in. centres, ½ in. pegs.
Height, 10½ in. (Bail adds 1 in.) Weight 12½lb.
Burner No. 46 (⅜ ft.). Carbide capacity 10 ozs. Burns about 4½ hours (each charge).

No.	Front. Glass.	Finish.		
XL186	781	9½ in.	8 in.	Ebony Black (Plated Parts) £13 4 0
XL187	783	,,	,,	,, (Brass Parts) £13 4 0
XL188	784	,,	,,	All Brass ... 13 4 0
XL189	786	,,	,,	All Plated ... 14 0 0

Medium Size.

Fits Standard Brackets, 7¼ in. centres, ½ in. pegs.
Height, 10 in. (Bail adds 1⅛ in.) Weight 12 lb.
Burner No. 44 (⅔ ft.) Carbide capacity 8 oz. Burns about 3½ hours (each charge).

No.	Front. Glass.	Finish.		
XL190	791	7¾ in.	6¾ in.	Ebony Black (Plated Parts) £10 15 0
XL190A	793	,,	,,	,, (Brass Parts) £10 15 0
XL190B	794	,,	,,	All Brass 10 15 0
XL190C	796	,,	,,	All Plated ... 11 5 0

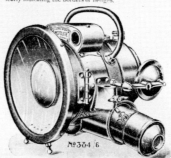

Nos. 384 and 386. **THE "MOTOLITE."**

Height 10 in. (Bail adds 1 in.) Weight 9 lbs.
Front 8½ ins. Glass 7¼ ins. Lens 3½ ins.
Burns 4 hours.

XL193	No. 384. All Brass ...	£8 10 0
XL193A	No. 386. All Nickel-plated ...	9 0 0

Front, 8 in. Glass, 6¾ in.
Fits Standard Brackets (7¼ in. centres, ½ in. pegs).
Height, 9 in. (Bail adds 1½ in.) Weight 10 lb.
Burner No. 44 (⅔ ft.).
Carbide capacity, 10 oz.
Burns 4½ hours.
XL191 N51 Ebony Black (Plated Parts) £8 10 0
XL191A N53 Ebony Black (Brass Parts) £8 10 0
XL192 N54 All Brass £8 10 0
XL192A N56 All Plated £9 0 0

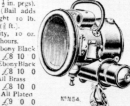

THE "KINGLITE."
New Model for 1911.

No. N54.

"AUTOLITE."

Height 10½ ins. Weight 8¾ lbs. Front 7¼ ins.
Lens 3 in. Burns 4 hrs.
XL194 No. 594. All Brass ... £7 10 0
XL194A No. 596. All Nickel plated £8 0 0

Nos. 594 and 596.

160

36. Another similar Powell & Hanmer self-contained brass acetylene head lamp. Mirrored concave reflectors, 4ins.:10cm diameter. 10ins.:25cm high. Circa 1910.

£60 — £100

35. A Powell and Hanmer No. 503 self-contained acetylene brass head lamp with 8ins.:20cm diameter front. Margin lens reflector (concave mirror). The slightly smaller model, No. 500, cost £2. 1. 6d. (£2.07½) in 1913.

£90 — £120

37. Produced by Powell and Hanmer in 1913 for use on the Morris Oxford, a pair of self-contained acetylene head lamps with carrying handles, plated brass, the maker's plate marked 'The Morris Oxford'. Glass diameter 5¼ins.:13.5cm, 9½ins.:24cm long, 10¼ins.:26cm high. Scarce as genuine pair, note hinges to front reservoir covers etc. Price each generally in 1913, £2. 5s. 6d. (£2.27½) nickel plated, £2. 1s. 6d. (£2.07½) brass.

£275 — £350 pair, very scarce marked 'The Morris Oxford'

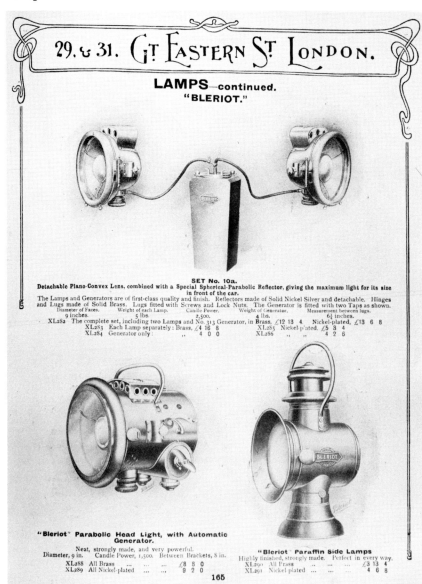

29. & 31. GT EASTERN ST. LONDON.

LAMPS—continued.
"BLERIOT."

SET No. 10a.

Detachable Plano-Convex Lens, combined with a Special Spherical-Parabolic Reflector, giving the maximum light for its size in front of the car.

The Lamps and Generators are of first-class quality and finish. Reflectors made of Solid Nickel Silver and detachable. Hinges and Lugs made of Solid Brass. Lugs fitted with Screws and Lock Nuts. The Generator is fitted with two Taps as shown.

Diameter of Faces.	Weight of each Lamp.	Candle Power.	Weight of Generator.	Measurement between lugs.
9 inches.	5 lbs.	2,500.	4 lbs.	6¼ inches.

XL282 The complete set, including two Lamps and No. 313 Generator, in Brass, £12 13 4. Nickel-plated, £13 6 8
XL283 Each Lamp separately: Brass, £4 16 8   XL285 Nickel-plated, £5 3 4
XL284 Generator only: „   4 0 0   XL286   „   4 2 6

"Bleriot" Parabolic Head Light, with Automatic Generator.

Neat, strongly made, and very powerful.
Diameter, 9 in.   Candle Power, 1,500.   Between Brackets, 8 in.
XL288 All Brass £8 8 0
XL289 All Nickel-plated 9 2 0

"Bleriot" Paraffin Side Lamps
Highly finished, strongly made. Perfect in every way.
XL290 All Brass £3 13 4
XL291 Nickel plated 4 6 8

165

38. The name of Bleriot is perhaps more associated with flying, however a range of motoring accessories is to be found bearing his name on many fine lamps produced between 1900-14; also in partnership with Salsbury for a period. Here shown is a pair of stirrup mounted acetylene head lights with generator. Further Bleriot products also shown.

39. A pair of H. & B. (Howes & Burley) projector acetylene motor head lamps, having 5¾ ins.:14.5cm lenses, with concave mirror reflectors and shown together with their separate H. & B. acetylene generator (incomplete). Circa 1913. Original price of generator, two guineas.
£150 — £200 as shown

40. "The light produced by these celebrated motor head lamps is vast, strong, penetrating, soft, clear and beautiful in every particular ... They are most cheerful companions for a night's drive", was the American manufacturer's claim for lamps of this make in a 1911 catalogue. This Rushmore product was available in various sizes, from 6ins. to 10ins.: 15cm to 25cm diameter, and priced from £3. 10s. 0d. (£3.50) to £11. 11s. 0d. (£11.55) and may be found in brass or nickel finish. (Operated by separate generator.)

£80 — £100

41. Similar lamp from the Rushmore range, note shorter burner stem for tall burner, i.e. Elta, Ceto and Beto types, and typically Rushmore slatted glass.

£80 — £100

42. An E.C.L. aluminium acetylene head lamp, 9ins.:23cm diameter lens, surface corrosion evident. Circa 1912.

£15 — £25

Left: 43. Bearing maker's name plate 'Troy Steele' Jarrott Ltd., Orchard Street, London W., this brass acetylene head lamp has a 8ins.:20cm diameter lens of four piece construction and polished aluminium reflector. Note screw and lock nut missing from bracket, as usual.

£80 — £100

Right: 44. A self-contained acetylene head lamp bearing 'WD' (War Department) impressed mark. Note double cylinders. This model was produced for the Army prior to or during the First World War, originally enamelled in khaki. Scarce and interesting.

£120 — £160

Lamps

45. Note the interesting reference to gas and electric variations to the Seabrook-Solar headlamps, presumably a transitional idea. Also illustrated are side and tail lamps, and generator. The instructive diagram shows carbide and water, the two essentials for production of acetylene gas.

46. A fine pair of brass electric side lamps by C.A.V. (Charles A. Vandervell & Co. London), 6ins. × 6ins.:15cm × 15cm. Bevelled and star cut lenses.
£150 — £200

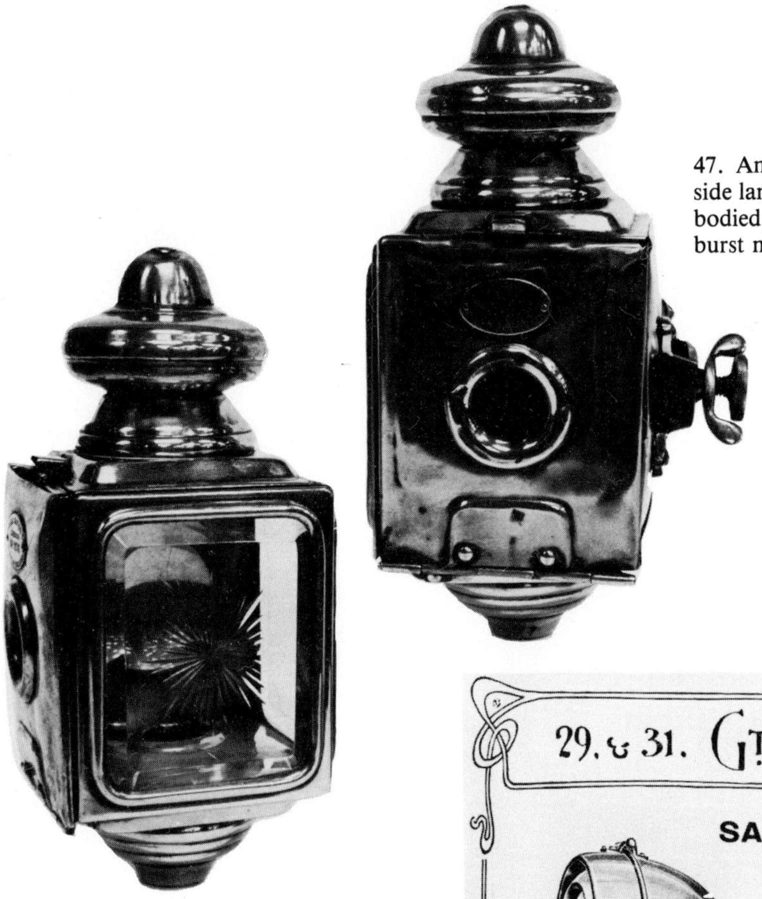

47. An attractive pair of 'Opera' type side lamps by Rotax, electric type, brass bodied, bevelled glasses with cut star-burst motifs, circa 1912.
£125 — £175

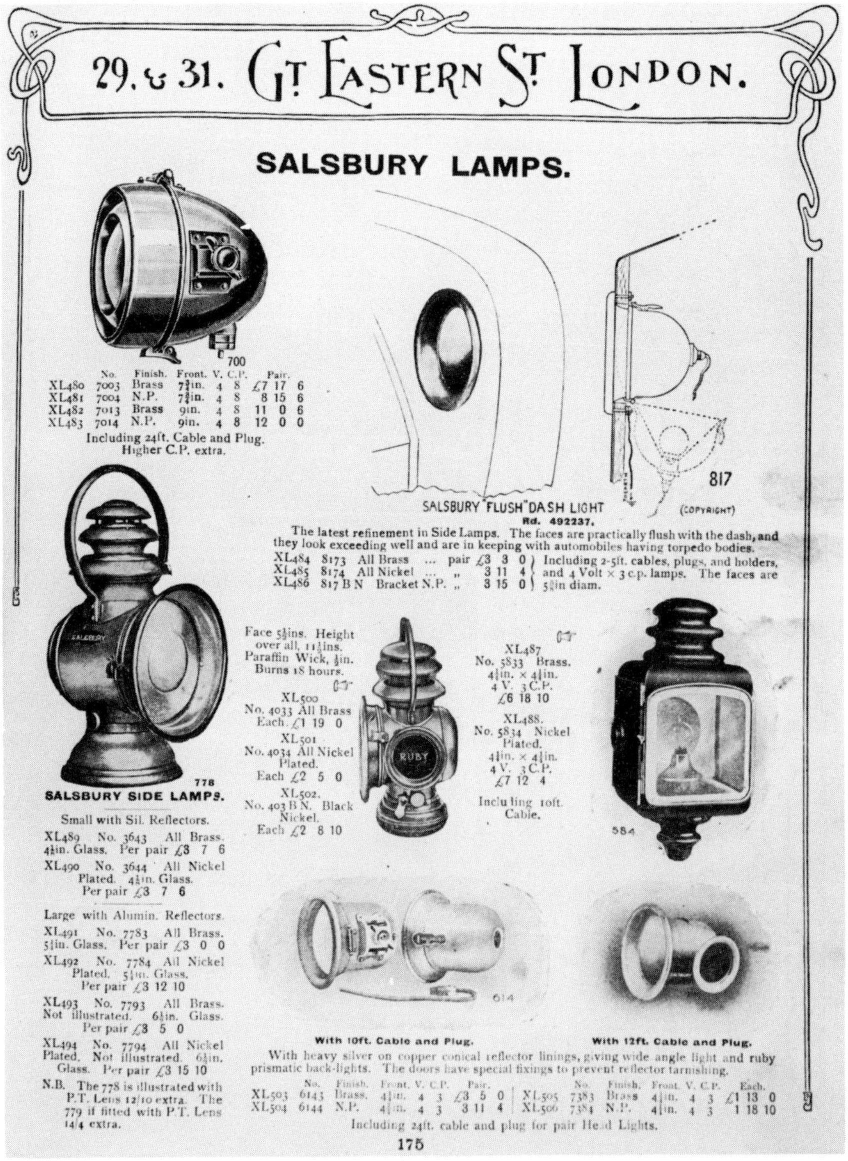

29. & 31. Gt Eastern St London.

SALSBURY LAMPS.

700

	No.	Finish.	Front.	V.	C.P.	Pair.
XL480	7003	Brass	7¾in.	4	8	£7 17 6
XL481	7004	N.P.	7¾in.	4	8	8 15 6
XL482	7013	Brass	9in.	4	8	11 0 6
XL483	7014	N.P.	9in.	4	8	12 0 0

Including 24ft. Cable and Plug.
Higher C.P. extra.

SALSBURY "FLUSH" DASH LIGHT
817
(COPYRIGHT)
Rd. 492237.

The latest refinement in Side Lamps. The faces are practically flush with the dash, and they look exceeding well and are in keeping with automobiles having torpedo bodies.

XL484	8173	All Brass ... pair	£3 3 0
XL485	8174	All Nickel ... „	3 11 4
XL486	817 B N	Bracket N.P. „	3 15 0

Including 2-5ft. cables, plugs, and holders, and 4 Volt × 3 c.p. lamps. The faces are 5⅝in diam.

778
SALSBURY SIDE LAMPS.

Small with Sil. Reflectors.
XL489 No. 3643 All Brass. 4½in. Glass. Per pair £3 7 6
XL490 No. 3644 All Nickel Plated. 4½in. Glass. Per pair £3 7 6

Large with Alumin. Reflectors.
XL491 No. 7783 All Brass. 5¼in. Glass. Per pair £3 0 0
XL492 No. 7784 All Nickel Plated. 5¼in. Glass. Per pair £3 12 10
XL493 No. 7793 All Brass. Not illustrated. 6¼in. Glass. Per pair £3 5 0
XL494 No. 7794 All Nickel Plated. Not illustrated. 6¼in. Glass. Per pair £3 15 10

N.B. The 778 is illustrated with P.T. Lens 12/10 extra. The 779 if fitted with P.T. Lens 14/4 extra.

Face 5½ins. Height over all, 11½ins. Paraffin Wick, ½in. Burns 18 hours.
XL500 No. 4033 All Brass Each £1 19 0
XL501 No. 4034 All Nickel Plated. Each £2 5 0
XL502. No. 403 B N. Black Nickel. Each £2 8 10

RUBY

XL487 No. 5833 Brass. 4¼in. × 4¼in. 4 V. 3 C.P. £6 18 10
XL488. No. 5834 Nickel Plated. 4¼in. × 4¼in. 4 V. 3 C.P. £7 12 4
Including 10ft. Cable.

584

614

With 10ft. Cable and Plug. With 12ft. Cable and Plug.

With heavy silver on copper conical reflector linings, giving wide angle light and ruby prismatic back-lights. The doors have special fixings to prevent reflector tarnishing.

	No.	Finish.	Front.	V.	C.P.	Pair.
XL503	6143	Brass.	4¼in.	4	3	£3 5 0
XL504	6144	N.P.	4¼in.	4	3	3 11 4

	No.	Finish.	Front.	V.	C.P.	Each.
XL505	7383	Brass	4¼in.	4	3	£1 13 0
XL506	7384	N.P.	4¼in.	4	3	1 18 10

Including 24ft. cable and plug for pair Head Lights.

175

48. Note the early flush mounted dash light suitable for 'automobiles having torpedo bodies', also the more 'modern' shaped side light products from the Salsbury range. Circa 1913.

50. A C.A.V. bell-shaped electric brass head lamp, stirrup mounting brackets visible. Circa 1915-20.
£25 — £40

49. Of unusual shape, these Salsbury electric side lamps have distinctive bulbous lenses with small ruby lens to rear centre. Bayonet electrical fittings enable lamps to be removed from vehicle for cleaning, simple socket from lug. Circa 1914.

£100 -- £125

51. A Rotax 9ins.:23cm brass head lamp, originally painted the colour of the car, frosted glass partly obscuring vacuum operated dipping reflector. From a period when cars used dipping reflectors as opposed to double filament bulbs, and normally nearside head lamp dipped and offside head lamp was switched off. Circa 1930.
£15 — £25

52. Attractive with their moulded faceted lenses with bull's-eye centres, a pair of H. & B. brass bracket mounted electric side lamps No. 1009, hinge-up fronts, side brackets. 6ins.:15cm diameter. Circa 1920.
£100 — £130

53. A Lucas torpedo-shaped side light, lamp dismantles for access to bulb by undoing thumb screw at rear, bull's-eye lens. Circa 1920.

£15 — £20

54. A pair of C.A.V. electric side lights, not from an automobile but from an aeroplane. The windows to side accommodate colour filters for aerial recognition purposes.
£30 — £50

56. A pair of Lucas L74 brass 'bell' shaped stirrup mounted electric head lamps with 10ins.:25cm 'Difusa' frosted lenses, one stirrup mounting shown. 1920s.
£40 — £60

55. This stirrup mounted brass electric head lamp by C.A.V. has a 9ins.:23cm diameter lens, note taper to stirrup. 'Twenties.

£25 — £40

57. The central bulb mount bears the Marchal trademark on this unusually constructed electric head lamp, the rim and main body of aluminium with brass shell doubling as reflector, 8ins.:20cm diameter. 1920s.
£30 — £40

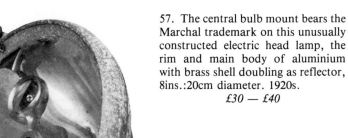

58. Another Marchal electric head lamp, this time incorporating bull's-eye reflector on central bar (provisions for two bulbs, Marchal emblem missing). 8¾ins.:22.5cm diameter. Late 'twenties.
£30 — £40

59. One of the high quality lamps available from the late 'twenties was the Stephen Grebel range, note distinctive plain lens with named centre. This lamp featured a rearward facing bulb held by internal supports, and was an attempt to produce improved lighting. Seen on high quality automobiles.
£100 — £125 each
£250 — £400 pair

61. A Stephen Grebel plated spot lamp, again of rounded form, swivelling on ball mount with bracket. Note etched Stephen Grebel trademark to centre of lens, overall diameter 9½ins.:24cm. Circa 1930.
£125 — £200

60. Considered by many to be the finest of vintage electric head lamps, this fine quality Stephen Grebel plated head lamp of rounded form has rearward facing bulb and plain slightly convex lens, overall diameter 11ins.:28cm. Circa 1930.
£125 — £150 each   £300 — £400 pair

62. Manufactured by Rushmore, this brass no. 926 electric hand operated spot lamp is mounted on revolving stirrup with bracket allowing unrestricted direction of beam. For use on large vehicles, e.g. fire engines, breakdown lorries, etc. 10¾ins.:27.5cm diameter. 'Twenties.

£50 — £75

63. This long range projector bi-flex type electric head lamp by Lucas numbered LBD 165 has chromium plated shell and 9½ins.:24cm diameter lens. 1930s.

£8 — £12

64. A pair of H. & H. nickel plated electric side lamps, reg. no. 541958, side mounting brackets, 4ins.:10cm diameter. Circa 1910-20.
£30 — £40

65. A pair of 1930s 'Tiltray' American chromium plated electric head lamps, optically influenced lens design, conical body. 10ins.:25cm diameter lens. Circa 1935.
£35 — £50

66. This Lucas produced FT 37 lamp was intended as a fog lamp and/or anti-dazzle pass light. The pass light was a pre-equivalent of our head lamp 'flasher' and could be supplied with a special silent signalling control switch resembling a horn button for zones of silence. Available in chrome or ebony black finish at £2. 9s. 6d. (£2.47½) in 1937.
£30 — £50

67. Introduced in November 1929, a pair of Lucas P.80 electric head lamps with reeded lenses, central reflectors mounted on triple bars, top hinged front bearing Lucas trademark. Lamps of this type were fitted to small Rolls-Royces, 1½ litre SS Jaguars etc. 10½ins.:27cm diameter lenses. Circa 1938.

£60 — £100

68. Incorporating a new feature for 1929, a pair of Lucas P.100 chromium plated head lamps (introduced October 1927), 'hinge-up' fronts with triple bar bulb mounting incorporating bull's-eye. Two bulbs, one mounted behind bull's-eye, the other (rearward facing) centrally on to reflector, frosted glass lower part fluted, with clear areas to centre and bull's-eye. 12ins.:30.5cm diameter overall. 'Thirties.
£200 — £350

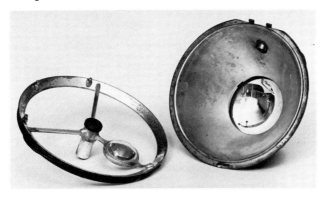

69. A dismantled P.100 head lamp showing reflector with central concave glass mirror and mounting for central bulb and bull's-eye.

70. Showing frosted and fluted glass as mentioned previously, but with bull's-eye, a pair of Lucas P.100 head lamps using one rearward facing centrally mounted bulb. In 1928 a pair of P.100s in ebony black finish cost £21; nickel plated £22; silver plated £30. The P.100 was at the top of the extensive Lucas range. 'Thirties.

£200 — £300

71. A later pair of Lucas P.100 head lamps, ebony black finish, this time having forward facing bulb, solenoid dipping reflector and triple bar mounted hood. Late 'thirties.
£125 — £200

72. A pair of post-war P.100 head lamps, hinge-down fronts, frosted glass with clear centre, dished triple bar mounted hood and modified chromium plated shell. 12ins.:30.5cm diameter.
£80 — £150

74. A similar pair to no. 73, this time with alternative finish of black painted shells and chrome rims. £9. 18s. 0d. (£9.90) in 1937.

£40 — £60

73. A pair of Lucas Long Range projector head lamps RB 170S, 10⅜ins.:27cm fronts with Biflex vertical bar reflector, chromium plated shells. Mid-'thirties. In 1937 retail price £11.

£50 — £75

75. A fine chromium plated Lucas spot lamp with frosted glass, plain centre, rearward facing bulb and hinge-up front. Sometimes used as centre lamp with P.100s, note similarity of design. Circa 1930.

£50 — £75

76. Again from the extensive Lucas range, a pair of fog lamps with fluted glass, horizontally divided reflectors, chromium plated. Early 'thirties.

£50 — £80

77. Intended for use on a Bentley car, this Lucas centre lamp has reeded glass horizontally divided reflector and vertical bar mounted hood incorporating the letter 'B', just visible. 'Thirties.

£40 — £60

78. An oval shaped fog lamp. Slightly convex clear reeded lens, chromium plated rim, black painted shell. Note simple mounting bracket allowing adjustment. Circa 1935.
£10 — £15

79. A pair of large size Lucas side lamps with emblem visible on reflector, lightly frosted glass with clear centre. Shown here with mounting bases. Sometimes used in conjunction with P.100s. 'Thirties.
£50 — £80

80. Produced by Lucas and C.A.V. (amalgamated 1926) with slight variations, this pair of side lamps have twist-off, reeded glass fronts, and are finished in black. 'Thirties.
£25 — £35

81. A pair of early post-war Lucas side lamps intended for use with their P.100s. Note red Lucas tell-tale panel at top of lamp indicating to driver that light is operating.
£30 — £40

82. A pair of Lucas 1130 streamlined side lamps, 1⅝ins.:4cm diameter, frosted glass, circular Lucas emblem warning panel. Chromium plated finish. Intended for use on sports cars. Mid-to late 'thirties.
£25 — £40

83. This Lucas 'STOP' tail and reversing lamp (No. 312L) has particular interest to owners of SS100 sports cars, etc. Prior to Second World War these lights were fitted singly as original equipment combining their mentioned features with number plate lights. When in the 'fifties lighting regulations required the fitting of two tail lights, many such lights were discarded in favour of more modern lights. Recently, however, the quest for originality has considerably enhanced the value of this lamp and they are now fitted in pairs, though it is of course necessary to reverse larger lenses around to produce symmetrical appearance.

£80 — £120 each

84. With the advent of blackout restrictions in the Second World War, all vehicles were required to use one form or another of dimming device to prevent lights being detected from the air. A range of head lamp masks was developed; shown left is a Lucas 'Maxlite' mask replacing original lamp rim and glass. This type was adopted for military use, shown above.

£5 — £8

85. In excellent condition, a head lamp mask by V. Hartley, in lightweight sheet steel.

£4 — £6

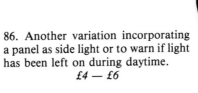

86. Another variation incorporating a panel as side light or to warn if light has been left on during daytime.

£4 — £6

Horns, Mirrors, Clocks and Dashboard Instruments

HORNS: Before the universal use of electricity, bulb horns and hand klaxons were the audible means of approach. Many types will be encountered, including intricate multi-coil types, boa constrictors, sometimes with fabulous serpents' heads, trumpets, and finished in polished brass, nickel plate, enamel and later chromium plate. Motor driven klaxons produced a distinctive note. Also to be noted are exhaust horns operated by directing exhaust gas through a whistle.

Towards the late 'thirties, some horns had disappeared under the bonnet and become utilitarian.

MIRRORS: A variety of externally mounted mirrors was available from the early days, normally in brass or nickel plated frames with bevelled mirrored glass. They were often mounted on stout supports, necessitated by bumpy roads and harsh suspension. In the 'twenties, with the popularity of closed cars, mirrors became more of an internal feature and those to the exterior were often mounted on the wings and were generally of rather simple form.

CLOCKS AND DASHBOARD INSTRUMENTS: With the early speed limits, a speedometer was essential and many varieties existed, usually mounted low on the dashboard or on the steering column, often driven from a front wheel. Gradually other instruments, notably clocks, were introduced, usually of detachable Goliath watch type mounted at an angle to enable ease of reading. Other aids, e.g. pressure and fuel gauges, ammeters, etc. became standard in the 'twenties.

87. A selection of early multi-coil motor horns c.1911, three having flexible connections, enabling horn to be mounted to exterior of vehicle, the bulb normally being attached to steering column. Rubber bulbs and connections have often perished but replacements are readily available. Upper right horn is of French manufacture with flexible metal connection.

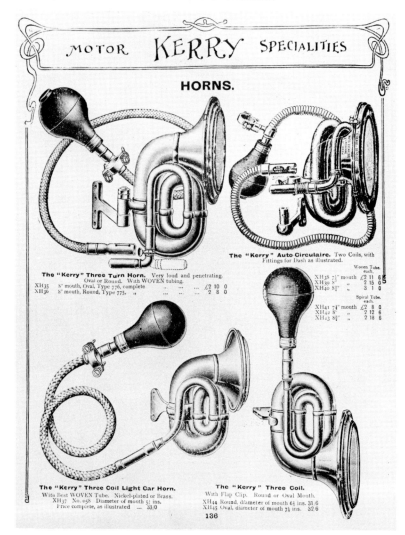

88. A Rubes upright brass single coil bulb horn, oval trumpet with detachable mesh grille, rubber bulb missing. Circa 1915.
£15 — £25

89. Two similar oval mouthed brass bulb horns, extensions and bulbs missing. Double coil (left), single coil (right). Both circa 1910.
£15 — £25 each

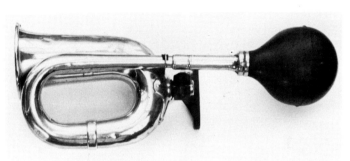

90. A Lucas No. 34 nickel plated single coil bulb horn with simple mounting bracket. 16¼ins.:41cm long overall. 1920s.
£25 — £35

91. Black painted with brass trumpet, this small double coil bulb horn has mounting bracket just visible. 13ins.:33cm long. 1920s.
£25 — £30

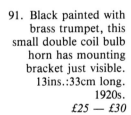

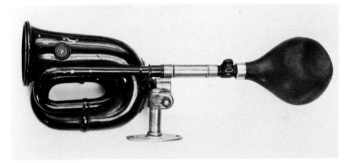

92. A Lucas 'King of the Road' No. 38 double coil bulb horn showing adjustable mounting bracket, black painted finish nickel fittings. 1920s.
£30 — £40

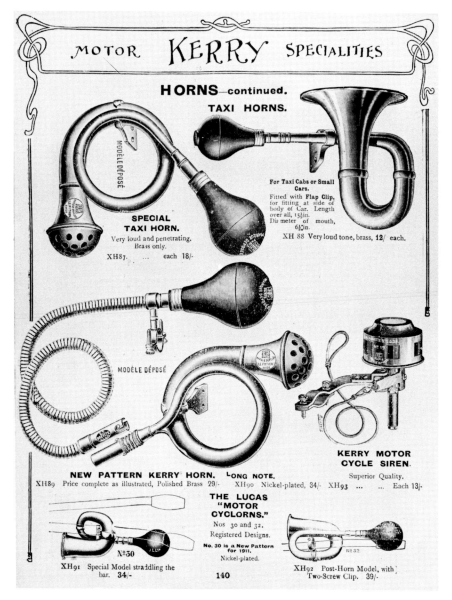

93. Described as taxi horns, top left, with perforated dome cover to mouth of horn and, below, a horn of similar form, this time with similar connection. The siren and horns at bottom of the Kerry sales catalogue are for motor cycles.

Below left: 94. A 'Desmo' double coil bulb horn, bulb missing. 'Desmo' produced a wide range of competitively priced motoring accessories. 1920s.
£25 — £35

Below right: 95. Produced by H & S and bearing 'Silverdale' trademark, a simple bulb horn. 1920s.
£15 — £25

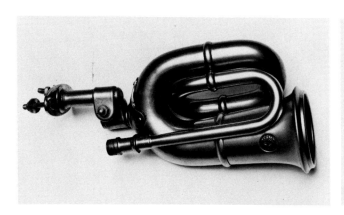

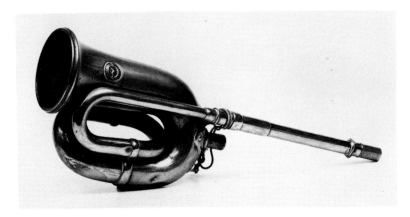

96. A Lucas 'King of the Road' No. 38 brass double coil bulb horn with wire mesh grille to mouth of trumpet clearly visible, bulb missing. 1920s.

£20 — £30

97. Having coiled interior to trumpet, this Lucas bulb horn is of brass construction, with bracket and replacement bulb. 22ins.:56cm long overall. 1920s.

£15 — £25

98. Of simple form, this Desmo scuttle mounted bulb horn is of all brass construction. 20ins.:51cm long. 1920s.

£15 — £20

99. This type of bulb horn was fitted through the dash. Brass trumpet, note bulb beginning to perish. 1920s.

£15 — £25

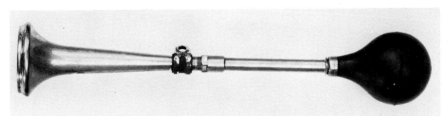

100. Another 'Desmo' straight bulb horn of brass construction, part of mounting clamp visible. 20½ins.:52cm long. 1920s.

£12 — £18

101. Another dash mounted bulb horn by Lucas, a type often seen on taxis. Usual perishing to original bulb, mesh cover missing.

£12 — £18

102. A Lucas 'King of the Road' black enamelled bulb horn, shown here complete with mounting bracket. Circa 1930. Many rubber bulbs have perished but replacements are still being manufactured.

£25 — £30

103. By unusual maker, Dekla of Birmingham, this bulb horn shown here with extension piece to facilitate accessibility of bulb. Circa 1930.

£15 — £20

104. An unusual chromium plated brass double coiled bulb horn of French manufacture, with attractively perforated cover. A similar horn was available in 1913 with flexible woven extension, this model shortened. Circa 1930.

£25 — £35

105. With enamelled black finish a double coil trumpet horn with flexible nickel plated extension to bulb. This model known as 'Rotax Clarion'. Circa 1930.

£25 — £35

106. A fine large brass boa constrictor horn, trumpet diameter 8¼ins.:21cm, complete with fine mesh, mounting bracket clearly visible, tapering flexible extension. Circa 1915.   *£100 — £150*

107. A small boa constrictor horn, nickel plated trumpet (lacking mesh) and tapering flexible extension. 50ins.:127cm long overall.   *£75 — £90*

108. Scarce with the coiled trumpet, this boa constrictor bulb horn is in polished brass. 59ins.:150cm long overall.   *£60 — £100*

109. A fine example of a boa constrictor bulb horn with flared trumpet, 5ins.:13cm diameter, mounting bracket visible and chromium plated finish. 47¼ins.:120cm long overall. Circa 1930. This type of horn had a long production life. Circa 1910-40.   *£75 — £90*

110. Larger than the previous example, this boa constrictor bulb horn has a 8ins.:20cm diameter trumpet, flexibility of tapered connection clearly visible, polished brass. 82ins.:208cm long overall. A 1911 catalogue lists similar models in brass at £5.   *£100 — £150*

111. A similar boa constrictor bulb horn to 110, this time with chromium plated finish. 1930s. This model originally cost £7. 9s. 0d. (£7.45), nickel plated at £5. 10s. 0d. (£5.50).   *£100 — £150*

112. Possibly the most desirable form of boa constrictor horns are those with a serpent's head with its jaws open, forked tongue protruding and glass eyes. Brass construction, tapering flexible extension. 76½ins.:193cm long overall. Probably 1930s. (See also catalogue illustration below).   *£120 — £160*

113. Note the serpent's head model boa horn, still being produced in the late 1930s, further boa horns and a Lucas double turn horn. 1937.

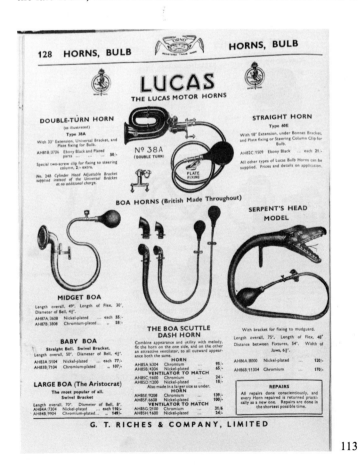

113

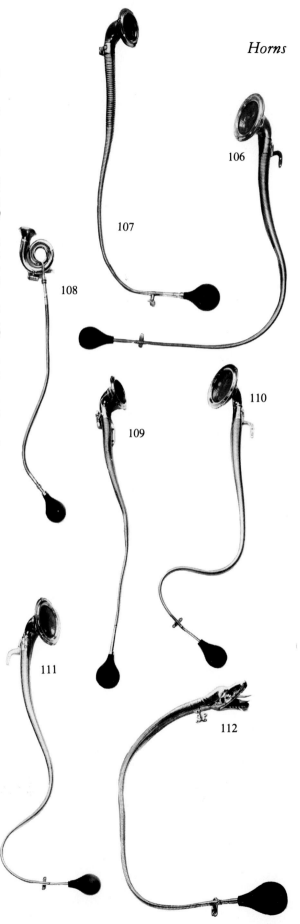

106

107

108

109

110

111

112

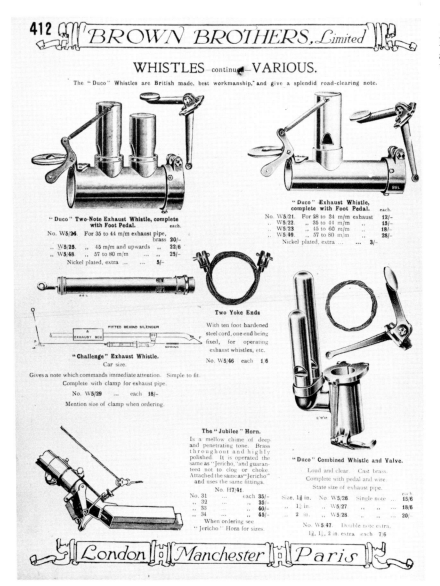

412 BROWN BROTHERS, Limited

WHISTLES—continued—VARIOUS.

The "Duco" Whistles are British made, best workmanship, and give a splendid road-clearing note.

"Duco" Two-Note Exhaust Whistle, complete with Foot Pedal.

No. W5/24.	For 35 to 44 m/m exhaust pipe, brass	each. 20/-
„ W5/25.	„ 45 m/m and upwards „	22/6
„ W5/48.	„ 57 to 80 m/m „	25/-
	Nickel plated, extra	5/-

"Challenge" Exhaust Whistle. Car size.

Gives a note which commands immediate attention. Simple to fit.
Complete with clamp for exhaust pipe.

No. W5/29 ... each 18/-

Mention size of clamp when ordering.

"Duco" Exhaust Whistle, complete with Foot Pedal.

No. W5/21.	For 28 to 34 m/m exhaust	each. 12/-
„ W5/22.	„ 35 to 44 m/m „	13/-
„ W5/23.	„ 45 to 60 m/m „	18/-
„ W5/49.	„ 57 to 80 m/m „	28/-
	Nickel plated, extra ...	3/-

Two Yoke Ends

With ten foot hardened steel cord, one end being fixed, for operating exhaust whistles, etc.

No. W5/46 each 1/6

The "Jubilee" Horn.

Is a mellow chime of deep and penetrating tone. Brass throughout and highly polished. It is operated the same as "Jericho," and guaranteed not to clog or choke. Attached the same as "Jericho" and uses the same fittings.

No. 31	...	each	35/-
„ 32	...	„	35/-
„ 33	...	„	40/-
„ 34	...	„	43/-

When ordering see "Jericho" Horn for sizes.

"Duco" Combined Whistle and Valve.

Loud and clear. Cast brass.
Complete with pedal and wire.
State size of exhaust pipe.

Size, 1¼ in.	No W5/26	Single note ...	each 15/6
„ 1½ in.	„ W5/27	„	18/6
„ 2 in.	„ W5/28	„	20/-
No. W5/47.	Double note extra.		
1¼, 1½, 2 in. extra		each 7/6

London Manchester Paris

114. On the same theme as the exhaust horn, a selection of sirens and whistles available in Brown Brothers' pre-World War I catalogue.

115. A simple brass 'Tentophone' exhaust gas operated whistle (sometimes known as sirens). Driver's control of valve allowed operation at will. Circa 1910.

£30 — £50

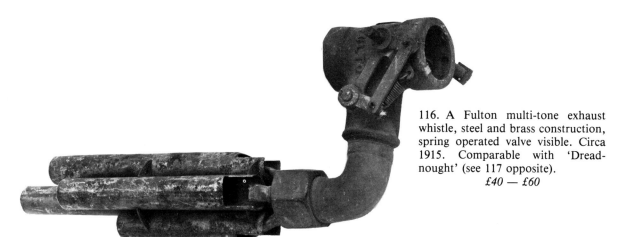

116. A Fulton multi-tone exhaust whistle, steel and brass construction, spring operated valve visible. Circa 1915. Comparable with 'Dreadnought' (see 117 opposite).
£40 — £60

117. Further exhaust whistles, and a 'Dreadnought' three note siren.

118. Something of a novelty, this Birdie 'Cuckoo' horn produced by Northumbrian Products, was fitted under the bonnet. 51ins.:20cm high. Shown also with instructions and original damp damaged box. 1930s.
£20 — £30

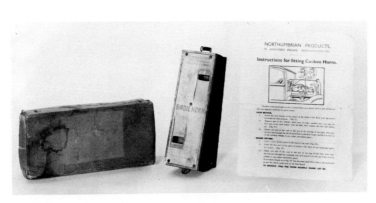

119. A brass 'Giro' hand plunger operated klaxon type horn. 9¼ins.:23.5cm long. Circa 1920.
£40 — £50

120. As an alternative to the more conventional front mounted horn, exhaust horns were produced in some quantity. Top, the 'Gabriel' exhaust horn; centre, early pattern electric horn by 'Ever-Ready', note 4 to 6 or 8 volts; below, a selection of small Lucas bulb horns.

MOTOR **KERRY** SPECIALITIES

HORNS –continued.

THE "GABRIEL" HORN.

XH54· Size 2. 2½in.×30in. £6 0 0 each.
XH55 ,, 3. 3in.×32in. 8 7 0 ,,
XH56 ,, 4. 3½in.×33in. 11 14 0 ,,
EXTRA F   PLATING 10 –.

Actuated by the Exhaust, and controlled by small pedal. Fits any Car. All sizes in stock.

Please state size of Exhaust Pipe when ordering.

Total length over all, 19½ ins. Fitted with two special Spring Terminals on Horn, which make it impossible for connecting wires to drop out.

Illustration of special "Ever-Ready" Waterproof Push for steering wheel.

XH57 **The "KERRY" SYREN.**
Very Loud and Powerful.
SIZE OF BELL, 8 in.
Price complete, with Cable and Attachment for Clutch, £6

The "EVER-READY" ELECTRIC CAR HORN.

The great feature of this Horn is the special form of condenser with which it is fitted, which prevents "pitting" of the platinum contacts and almost entirely obviates the necessity of any adjustments. Should, however, any adjustment become necessary in course of time, it can be effected by turning a milled nut by hand without the use of any tool.

This new "Ever-Ready" Horn is constructed on thoroughly scientific principles, giving a loud and penetrating yet inoffensive note, with a low consumption of electric energy.

XH58 Type 1092. 4 to 6 Volts. Horn Trumpet and Special
        Push. Polished Brass... £4 2 6
XH59 Ditto, Nickel-plated 4 6 0
XH60 Type 1093. 8 Volts. Horn Trumpet and Special
        Push. Polished Brass £4 14 6
XH61 Ditto, Nickel-plated 4 18 0

LUCAS.

"KING OF THE ROAD."
Single Turn.
XH66 No. 34, with Extension, brass, each £2 11 0
XH67 Ditto, ditto, plated ... ... each £2 11 0

"KING OF THE ROAD," with Extensions.
XH62 No. 42, with G. Bracket, brass, each £3 4 0
XH63 Ditto, Ditto, N.P. 3 4 0

"KING OF THE ROAD."
Post Horn Model, without Extension.
XH64 No. 34S, with screw clip, brass, each £1 19 0
XH65 Ditto, plated ,, 1 19 0

"KING OF THE ROAD."
Double Turn, with Extension.
XH68 No. 38, brass, each £3 0 0
XH69 Ditto plated ,, 3 0 0

"KING OF THE ROAD."
Half Turn Pattern, for outside driver's seat.
XH70 No. 40, brass, each £2 8 6
XH71 Ditto, plated ,, 2 8 6

138

121. The 'Godric' electric motor horn carried a provisional patent for 1908. All brass construction, trumpet diameter 7¾ins.:19.5cm, complete with mounting bracket. Edwardian.
£50 — £70

122. A large and impressive brass 'klaxon' horn available in either 8 or 12 volt, integral mounting bracket. Circa 1915. (In 1913 this model was available from £7. 7s. 0d. to £8. 7s. 0d. (£7.35-£8.35) depending on voltage and finish.)
£50 — £70

123. This 12 volt electric C.A.V. horn is similar in appearance to a klaxonet oval mouthed brass trumpet with enamelled black body. 11¼ins.:28.5cm long. Circa 1920.

£20 — £30

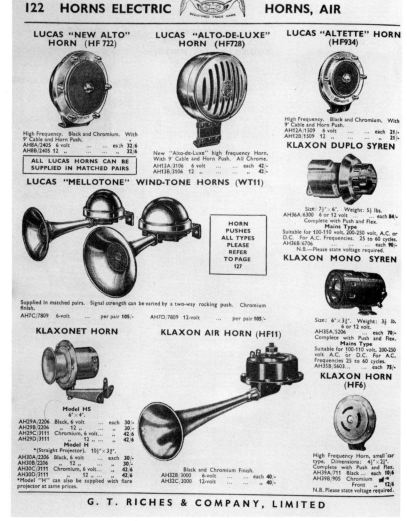

122 HORNS ELECTRIC *ORNO REGISTERED TRADE MARK* **HORNS, AIR**

LUCAS "NEW ALTO" HORN (HF 722)

LUCAS "ALTO-DE-LUXE" HORN (HF728)

LUCAS "ALTETTE" HORN (HF934)

High Frequency. Black and Chromium. With 9' Cable and Horn Push.
AH8A/2405   6 volt   ...   ...   ea:h 32/6
AH8B/2405 12 „   ...   ...   „   32/6

ALL LUCAS HORNS CAN BE SUPPLIED IN MATCHED PAIRS

New "Alto-de-Luxe" high frequency Horn. With 9' Cable and Horn Push. All Chrome.
AH13A/3106   6 volt   ...   ...   each 42/-
AH13B/3106 12 „   ...   ...   „   42/-

High Frequency. Black and Chromium. With 9' Cable and Horn Push.
AH12A/1509   6 volt   ...   ...   each 21/-
AH12B/1509 12 „   ...   ...   „   21/-

KLAXON DUPLO SYREN

Size: 7½" × 6". Weight: 5½ lbs.
AH36A/6300   6 or 12 volt   ...   ...   each 84/-
Complete with Push and Flex.
Mains Type
Suitable for 100-110 volt., 200-250 volt., A.C. or D.C. For A.C. Frequencies. 25 to 60 cycles.
AH36B/6706   ...   ...   each 90/-
N.B.—Please state voltage required.

LUCAS "MELLOTONE" WIND-TONE HORNS (WT11)

HORN PUSHES ALL TYPES PLEASE REFER TO PAGE 127

Supplied in matched pairs. Signal strength can be varied by a two-way rocking push. Chromium finish.
AH7C/7809   6-volt   ...   per pair 105/-
AH7D/7809 12-volt   ...   per pair 105/-

KLAXON MONO SYREN

Size: 6" × 3¾". Weight: 3½ lb.
6 or 12 volt.
AH35A/5206   ...   ...   each 70/-
Complete with Push and Flex.
Mains Type
Suitable for 100-110 volt, 200-250 volt. A.C. or D.C. For A.C. Frequencies 25 to 60 cycles.
AH35B/5603...   ...   each 75/-

KLAXONET HORN

KLAXON AIR HORN (HF11)

Model HS
6" × 4".
AH29A/2206   Black, 6 volt   ...   each 30/-
AH29B/2206   „   12   „   ...   „   30/-
AH29C/3111   Chromium, 6 volt...   „   42/6
AH29D/3111   „   12   „   ...   „   42/6
Model H
*(Straight Projector). 10⅜" × 3⅜".
AH30A/2206   Black, 6 volt   ...   each 30/-
AH30B/2206   „   12   „   ...   „   30/-
AH30C/3111   Chromium, 6 volt...   „   42/6
AH30D/3111   „   12   „   ...   „   42/6
*Model "H" can also be supplied with flare projector at same prices.

Black and Chromium Finish.
AH32B/3000   6-volt   ...   ...   each 40/-
AH32C/3000 12-volt   ...   ...   „   40/-

KLAXON HORN (HF6)

High Frequency Horn, small car type. Dimensions: 4½" × 2½". Complete with Push and Flex.
AH39A/711   Black   ...   each 10/6
AH39B/905   Chromium Front   „   12/6
N.B. Please state voltage required.

G. T. RICHES & COMPANY, LIMITED

126. A selection of externally mounted horns available in the late-1930s. The Lucas horns shown here were available in 6 or 12 volt. The 'Alto-de-luxe' and 'Mellotone' were often mounted in pairs.

Below: 124. A 6 volt klaxonet model H, a later type model finished in grey with manufacturer's plate and bracket clearly visible, advertised in 1937 at 30s. (£1.50). 10½ins.:26.5cm long.

£15 — £20

125. Claimed to be 'the finest horn in the Bosch range and one of the best on the market', this imported pre-War German product was available in black or chromium finish, shown here with Bosch switch and switch with mounting bracket. Circa 1935.

£15 — £25

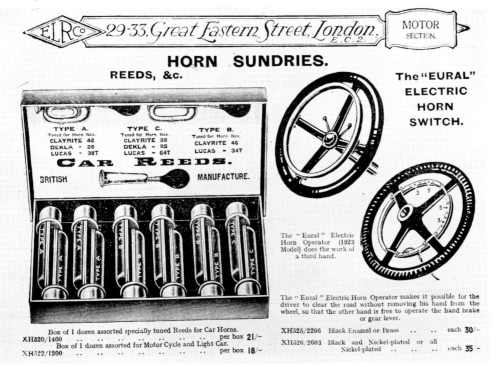

127. The "Eural" Electric Horn Operator and selection of bulb horn needs from 1923 E.L.R. Co. motor catalogue.

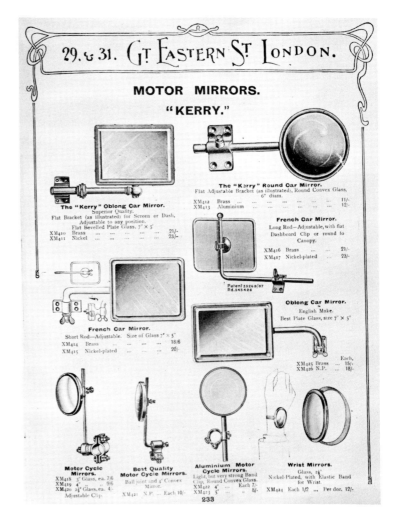

128. A selection of early mirrors in a variety of frames, note the unusual 'wrist mirror' lower right. Circa 1912.

129. Windscreen pillar-mounted circular mirror employing simple bracket made from two pieces of flat brass, bevelled edge to glass. Circa 1912.

£30 — £45

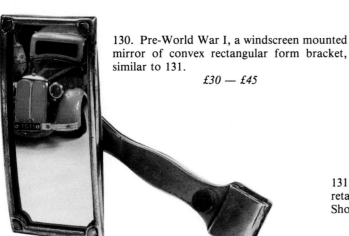

130. Pre-World War I, a windscreen mounted mirror of convex rectangular form bracket, similar to 131.

£30 — £45

131. An Oldfield 'Dependence' mirror of pre-World War I retains traces of original nickel plating, practically made. Shown here with its support.

£40 — £50

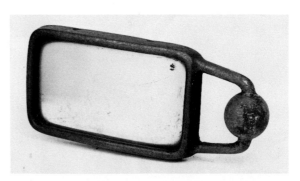

133. Another cast aluminium commercial vehicle mirror of rectangular shape with twin arms supporting ball. 6ins.:15cm wide. 1920s.

£5 — £10

132. Of cast aluminium body, this commercial vehicle rear view exterior circular mirror has simple but effective ball and socket mounting. 1920s.

£5 — £10

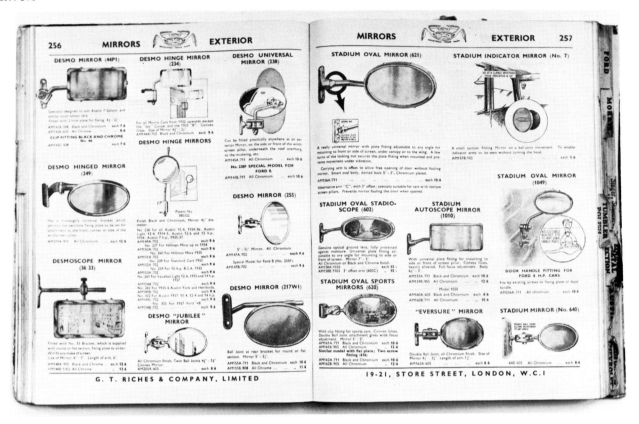

134. A selection of 1930s exterior mirrors by Desmo, Stadium, etc. Note interesting indicator mirror, top right.

135. A further variation of an exterior mirror utilising ball and socket mounting principle.
£5 — £10

136. Utilising a clamp for mounting, a standard aluminium framed exterior mirror, Pennant trade mark. 1920s.
£5 — £10

137. From the 1930s, a Desmo chromium plated wing mirror with cranked arm. 4½ins.:11.5cm diameter.
£5 — £10

138. A selection of interior mirrors from the Riches 1937 catalogue, basic designs from the Desmo, 'Orno', Stadium and Eversure factories.

MIRRORS   *ORNO* REGISTERED TRADE MARK   **INTERIOR** 251

"ORNO" FLAT OVAL INTERIOR MIRROR

With bevelled edges. Ball type Bracket with Universal adjustment. Size 7" × 2¼".
AM100A/203 ... ... each 3/-

"ORNO" INTERIOR MIRROR

Interior Flat Mirror. 7½" × 2¼". Bevelled edges.
AM103A/111 ... ... each 2/6

DESMO INTERIOR MIRROR (256)

Fitted with Ball Joint Bracket. 7" × 3".
AM106A/305 ... ... each 4/6

EVERSURE INTERIOR MIRROR (113)

3¼" × 2" Convex Glass. Black and Chromium.
AM107A/309 ... ... each 5/-

"ORNO" BIJOU MIRROR

Bijou Sports Models. Plate Fitting. Bevelled edge Convex Mirror, giving true vision over a wide angle. Strong Fixing Bracket. Ball adjustment. Chromium Plated. Made in two sizes.
AM101A/201   Size 3½" × 1⅞"   ... each 2/9
AM101B/208   Size 4½" × 2"   ... ,, 3/6

"ORNO" BIJOU MIRROR

Bevelled edge Convex Mirror giving true vision over a wide angle. Ball adjustment, Chromium plated. Made in two sizes.
    3½" × 1⅞"
AM104A/201 ... ... each 2/9
    4½" × 2"
AM104B/208 ... ... each 3/6

DESMO BIJOU MIRROR (257)

Ball Joint Bracket.
AM108A/305 ... ... each 4/6

STADIUM BIJOU MIRROR (1028)

3½" × 1⅞". Chromium Finish.
AM102A/309 ... ... each 5/-

STADIUM FRAMELESS MIRROR (1040)

Ball Joint Bracket.   Plate Glass.   7½" × 2½"
AM105A/208   Plate Fitting   ... each 3/6
AM105B/208   Hook-over Clip ...   ,, 3/6

DESMO SMALL INTERIOR MIRROR (215)

Specially suitable for use on cars with small rear windows, or where compactness is desired. Size 3½" × 1⅞".
AM109B/208   Black and Chromium
    finish ... ... each 3/6
AM109C/305   All Chromium finish   ,, 4/6
      (221)
Fitted with flat glass and longer fixing plate. Specially suitable for Austin 7 and other light saloons. Size 4½" × 2½".
AM110B/402   Black and Chromium
    finish ... ... each 5/6
AM110C/411   All Chromium finish   ,, 6/6

19-21, STORE STREET, LONDON, W.C.1

139. An Edwardian angle mounted dashboard clock, nickel plated case housing removable eight-day Goliath type watch, incorporating seconds dial. Angle mounted instruments are from a period when dashboards were low in relation to seating.

£35 — £50

140. A good 'Duco' Swiss-made eight-day car clock, shown here with its angled mount, detachable for winding, brass case, enamelled dial. 2½ins.:6.5cm diameter. Circa 1910.

£35 — £50

141. From the 1913 Brown Brothers' catalogue selection of clocks. On most early automobiles the driver sat high in relation to the dashboard — hence the extended angled mountings. Those shown are from the less expensive range, note the alarm clock lower centre.

142. A good quality 'Watford' clock from World War I period, heavy brass case with bevelled glass, eight-day movement, button activated hand setting visible. This model was used in early British tanks.

£35 — £50

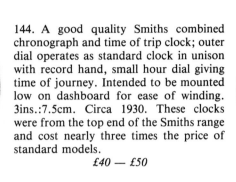

144. A good quality Smiths combined chronograph and time of trip clock; outer dial operates as standard clock in unison with record hand, small hour dial giving time of journey. Intended to be mounted low on dashboard for ease of winding. 3ins.:7.5cm. Circa 1930. These clocks were from the top end of the Smiths range and cost nearly three times the price of standard models.

£40 — £50

143. From the 1920s, another well-known make, this 'Watford' eight-day clock has silvered dial and bevelled glass, winder just visible on outside rim between 7 to 8 o'clock.

£15 — £20

145. A Smiths eight-day dashboard mounted car clock, silver face, obviously intended to be positioned low on dashboard by reason of fixed winder.

£12 — £18

146. An eight-day car clock with reeded aluminium bezel and front mounted winder, probably by Jaeger. Circa 1930.

£15 — £20

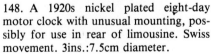

148. A 1920s nickel plated eight-day motor clock with unusual mounting, possibly for use in rear of limousine. Swiss movement. 3ins.:7.5cm diameter.

£8 — £12

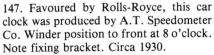

147. Favoured by Rolls-Royce, this car clock was produced by A.T. Speedometer Co. Winder position to front at 8 o'clock. Note fixing bracket. Circa 1930.

£35 — £50

149. A Smiths eight-day dashboard clock of dash mounted type, rim with serrations, similar to earlier rim wound version. Movement swings out on hinge to left to expose winder. 2¾ins.:7cm diameter. 1920s.

£12 — £18

150. This black faced Jaeger dashboard clock shows windows for illumination and flexible winder extension. From mid- to late 1930s.

£12 — £18

151. Note minor variations to design on these eight-day Smiths 'swing-out' car clocks, bezels similar to early rim wound versions. Circa 1928.
£12 — £18

152. A similar clock to above models, illustrating 'swing-out' body exposing winder, etc. Late 1920s.
£12 — £18

153. A Smiths eight-day dashboard clock, having swing-out front to expose winder, chromium plated. Circa 1930.
£15 — £20

154. A small flush mounted Smiths dashboard clock, 1¼ins.:5.5cm diameter, note cutaways to rim for illumination of face. Late 1930s.

£5 — £10

155. Having octagonal dial, this eight-day dash clock has flexible winder for ease of winding below dashboard. 1930s.

£20 — £30

156. A large eight-day clock of the type used in larger vehicles, this model from a Dennis motor coach. Note name to dial. 1930s.

£25 — £40

MOTOR **KERRY** SPECIALITIES

METERS.

STEWART SPEEDOMETERS.

GUARANTEED

FIVE YEARS.

XM358 Model 26. Three-inch dial, 60 mile Speedometer, 10,000 mile season odometer, automatic resetting trip register. £6 15 0

XM360 Model 10. Four-inch dial, 60 mile Speedometer, 10,000 mile season odometer, automatic resetting trip register, eight-day clock (keyless), electric light. £18 18 0

XM361 Model 29. Same as Model 10, but has 75 mile Speedomer. £23 12 6

XM362 Model 18. The same, except that it has 90 mile Speedometer ... £36 0 0

XM359 Model 11. Four-inch dial, 60 mile Speedometer, 10,000 mile season odometer, automatic resetting trip register. £7 17 6

XM363 Model 24. Three-inch dial, 50-mile Speedometer, 10,000 mile season odometer. £5 5 0

XM364 Model 28. Three-inch dial, 60 mile Speedometer, 10,000 mile season odometer, automatic resetting trip register, eight-day clock (keyless), electric light. £17 6 6

XM365 Model 32. Three inch dial, 60 mile Speedometer, 10,000 mile season odometer, automatic resetting trip register and watch £8 5 0

WHEN ORDERING please state Name and H.P. of Car, Size of Driving Wheel, and whether Brass or N.P. Finish.

XM366 Model 27. Four-inch dial, 75 mile Speedometer, 100,000 mile season odometer, automatic resetting trip register. £12 12 0

XM367 Model 19. Four-inch dial, 90 mile Speedometer, 100,000 mile season odometer, automatic resetting trip register. £23 12 6

228

157. Before the days of flush-fitted dashboard instruments, speedometers and clocks were mounted *on,* as opposed to *in,* the dashboard. They are attractive and usually well made. A 90 m.p.h. speedometer was available at a price of £23. 12s. 6d. (£23.63½). Some speedometers having electrical lighting were certainly a new innovation circa 1911. Shown here a range of American 'Stewart' speedometers. The suggestion of high workmanship is reflected in the offer of five years' guarantee.

158. Patented September 22nd 1908 and advertised 'The Gold Medal Speedometer' after their 1906 award in the speedometer trials, this Jones 60 m.p.h. speedometer has a distinctive dial and also incorporates mileometer and trip recorder. Price in 1911 £7. 17s. 6d. (£7.87½).

£30 — £45

159. Another Jones speedometer, this time with 50 m.p.h. dial, and mileage recorder, no trip meter, 3ins.:7.5cm diameter. Circa 1911.

£30 — £45

161. A veteran brass bodied speedometer incorporating trip and mileage display, 0-60 m.p.h., white face, bevelled glass.
£30 — £50

Above: 160. A Smiths bracket mounted 60 m.p.h. speedometer, silvered face incorporating mileage windows. Circa 1920.

£10 — £15

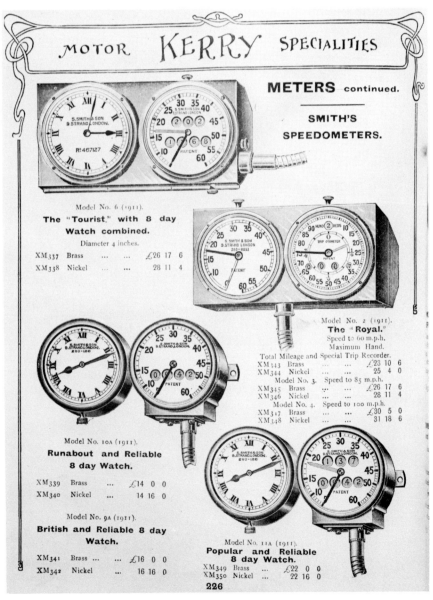

162. An interesting selection of instrument accessories by Smiths, including, top, eight-day watch and speedometer combination recording mileage and trip. Note 'light' coloured hand on speedometer is maximum hand to record maximum speed attained on journey in the same way as certain racing cars employed a recording hand on their revolution counters known as a 'telltale'. Centre right, speedometer with maximum hand and total mileage and special trip recorder. Centre left, a less sophisticated watch and speedometer. Below, watch and speedometer with trip recorder and maximum hand. Circa 1911.

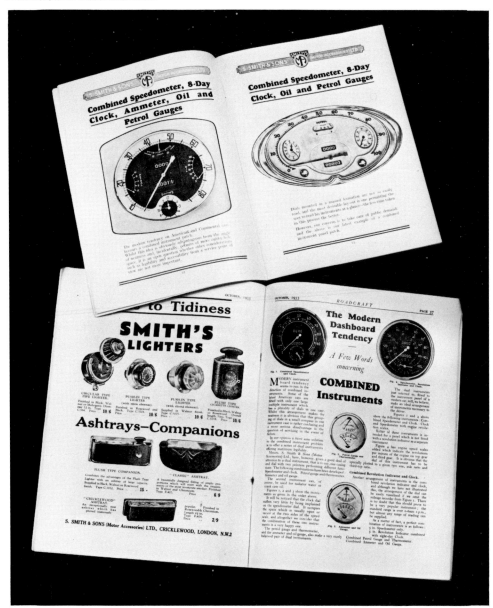

163. Two forms of advertisement for Smiths speedometers, at a period when it was popular to combine other instruments in the speedometer case. Above, from a Smiths catalogue; below, from *Roadcraft* magazine, 1933.

164. A Smiths 40 pounds per square inch silver faced oil pressure gauge, dashboard mounted. 2ins.:5cm diameter. 1920s.

£2 — £4

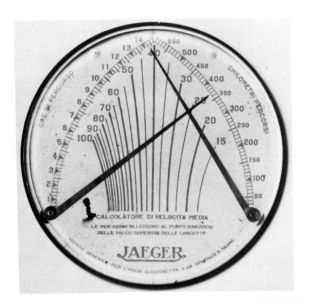

165. Of unusual design, an Italian 'Jaeger' average speed calculator showing time and distance pointers which indicated average speed at point of intersection. 3ins.:7.5cm diameter. 1930s.
£30 — £50

166. A 2,500 r.p.m. rev counter, black face marked 'Hudson Invader 168'. Circa 1930.
£10 — £15

167. A Smiths 2,500 r.p.m. rev counter, clockwise rotation. Note black face with caution area marked in red. 1930s.
£10 — £15

168. From a Rolls-Royce Phantom II Continental, a matched speedometer and revolution counter. Note, dual calibration on speedometer (m.p.h. and k.p.h.). Manufactured by A.T. Speedometer Co. Ltd. Early 'thirties.
£100 — £150 the pair

170. An early brass ignition switch, clearly marked 'ON OFF' for use on Thornycroft commercial vehicle. Circa 1920.

£2 — £4

169. On/off ignition switch of unusual form, contacts rotate through arc.

£2 — £4

171. A surprising number of variations exist for the simple switch, as this catalogue illustration indicates. We presume there are few collectors and these will be sought by those wishing to restore early dashboards. Note, below left, double ignition switch for changing over from magneto to coil and accumulator ignition. Self explanatory letters, e.g. M = magneto, A = accumulator.

Tools, Spares, Accessories and Clothing

There can be no doubt that earlier vehicles were more prone to breakdowns, the less serious of which could be remedied at the roadside if the driver had the knowledge and tools to effect a repair. Generally, many more tools and spares would be carried than nowadays, therefore it would not be surprising to find oil cans which were usually clipped on to the car, spare plugs, puncture outfits (punctures were regularly experienced due to poorer road surfaces and narrow sectioned high pressure tyres), etc., as well as the usual spanners, jack, tyre pumps, pressure gauges. A starting handle was an essential in the early days prior to self starters, after this they became a luxury and sometimes doubled as a wheel brace.

Manufacturers of automobiles produced their own tool kits with their name stamped on the shanks for use on their makes. Again, many of these items were marketed in attractively finished lithographed tins — again a popular area for the collector.

Sparking plugs were available in an enormous variety of shapes and finishes and often extremely well made, allowing for dismantling for cleaning. From the 'twenties onwards a standardisation began to take place under major makes.

Due to exposure to the elements and lack of proper heaters, etc., the early motorist was advised to wear special clothing; this notably took the form of coats, helmets and goggles. With the demise of the open car, such garments became less necessary.

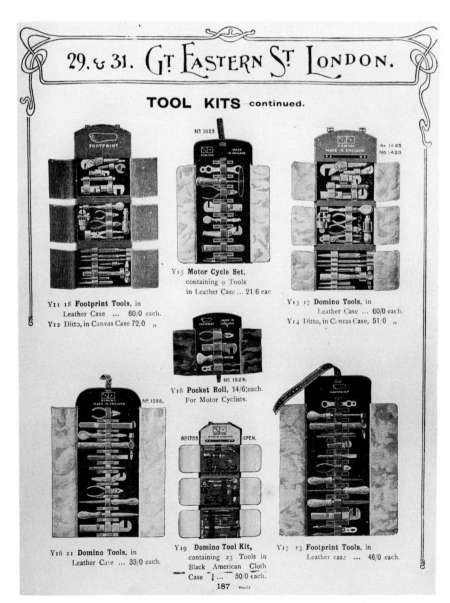

172. Before the motoring organisations became widespread, motorists had to be prepared to effect simple repairs to their automobiles and for this purpose tool kits and other such items were a necessity. From a pre-World War I catalogue, a selection of tool kits available, one containing as many as twenty-three tools all easily recognisable today.

174. A selection of tools, including three Austin marked spanners and a Morris valve spring compressor, another patent valve tool, and a Michelin tyre lever and rim tool. 'Twenties and 'thirties.

50p — £7

173. Tools can be collected for a variety of reasons. Still quite practical items, they may be collected for intriguing shapes, or for the names sometimes found stamped on them; included here 'Ford' and 'Fiat' stamped spanners, and a Taylors 'Quick Grip' plier.

50p — £3

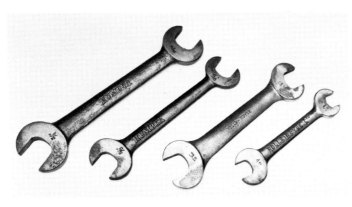

Above: 175. Further spanners bearing manufacturers' names: Humber and Rolls-Royce. 'Twenties and 'thirties.

£1 — £3

Above right: 176. A Humber ring spanner, a wheel rim tool, and a Vauxhall adjustable spanner (monkey wrench). 'Twenties and 'thirties.

£1 — £3

Right: 177. To save having to carry a multitude of small spanners the adjustable spanner quickly became popular. Above, one made by 'King Dick' which has been produced for a long period in virtually unchanged form and, below, a well-made competitor.

£1 — £3

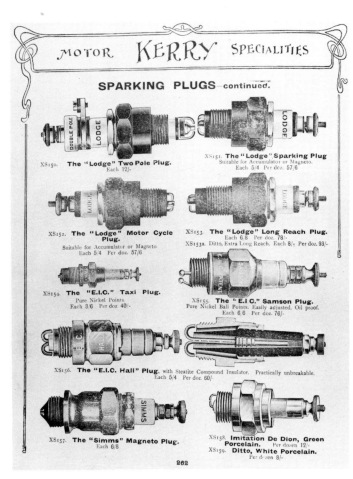

178. An interesting variety of sparking plugs which has helped to make this a potential area for the collector. Most early plugs, unlike those of today, could be easily dismantled for maintenance. Note the high price, when compared with today's price, and also various electrode types.

179. An early KLG plug (lower right hand corner), this time showing protective cover for electrode, gap setting instructions and guarantee, and hair spring type terminal fixing. Also shown, KLG plug in box with cardboard electrode protector, and a selection of KLG and Lodge boxes. 1920s.

£1 — £5

180. To illustrate the above point on maintenance, shown here is an early KLG plug dismantled for cleaning (a well-engineered item). Above it, an early Lodge plug (World War I period). The creator of the KLG sparking plug was Kenelm Lee Guinness, a successful racing driver. In the early 'twenties Guinness broke the land speed record at Brooklands in a 350 h.p. V12 Sunbeam.

£2 — £5

181. Shown here with its original bullet-shaped wooden box retaining portion of paper label and screw top marked 'Marque Déposée De Dion Bouton', this attractive brass, steel and white porcelain sparking plug also bears maker's initials DB. 3ins.:7.5cm long. Circa 1910.

£8 — £12

182. From left to right: a Lissen sparking plug of brass and mica construction; a Lodge 'Aero A5' brass, steel and mica plug with cooling fins, an attempt to prevent the possibility of pre-ignition, note unusual electrode; a KLG brass, steel and mica plug; a 'Rotor porcelain' insulated plug with steel body, and a Lissen H.1. steel, brass, copper and mica. All circa 1905-15.

£3 — £5

183. From left to right: an unusual brass bodied plug with composition insulator; a Bosch porcelain insulated steel bodied plug, note unusual electrodes; a KLG K.S.5 steel, brass, copper and mica plug; and a KLG type F steel, brass and mica plug. All circa 1910-20.

£3 — £5

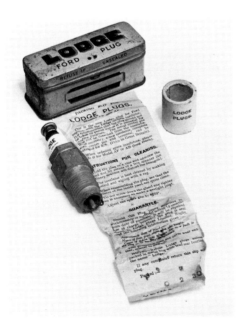

184. Lodge plug shown here with instruction leaflet mentioning that 'a new insulator complete with centrepin and terminal can be obtained for 2s. 6d (12½p)'. Note tapered thread for use on Fords.

£3 — £5

185. A Lodge 18mm sparking plug with cardboard electrode protector, and original tin, note price of 6s. (30p).

£2 — £3

186. Shown with its original tin, this Lodge sparking plug still carries its protective cardboard ferrule to thread. Mica insulator. Special tools were produced to dismantle some early plugs in order to clean or replace the central electrode, thus saving about 50% as the well-engineered casing would last almost indefinitely.

£2 — £3

187. Four long bodied Mica insulated plugs, mounted on brass carrier (this enabled driver to carry a spare set of plugs, usually conveniently stored under the bonnet). 'Twenties.

£10 — £12

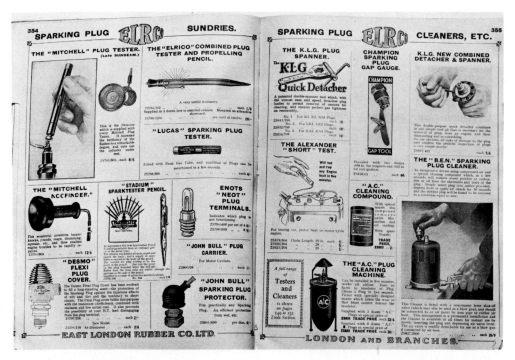

188. Catalogue selection of sparking plug testers, discussed below. Also note special KLG quick detacher used for dismantling plugs. Circa 1934.

189. Before the days of suppressor caps for sparking plugs, sparking plug testers were a useful tool. Shown here are two types, one with instructions. When applied to brass cap on plug terminal, flash was indicated by neon bulb and viewed through aperture, the brightness or weakness of flash determining condition of plug, circuit and points. 1930s.

£2 — £5

190. Various early garage jacks. The catalogue page is unusual in that it includes a 'visual' approach in an endeavour to explain operation. The interesting motor trolleys were used to assist movement of vehicles in confined spaces. Circa 1911.

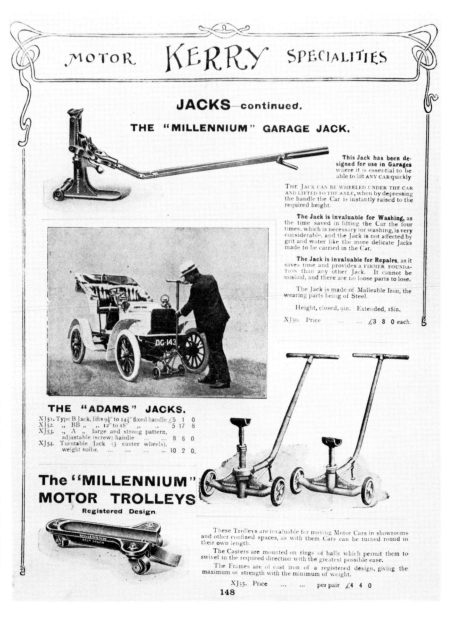

Below left: 191. A double-headed tyre gauge for commercial vehicles, of long form to enable dual rear tyres to be gauged, square section calibrated indicator with detachable valve key, here shown together with wooden storage case.

£5 — £8

Below right: 192. For use where gauges were not provided on the pump, a Schrader tyre pressure gauge calibrated to 100lbs. Early narrow sectioned tyres necessitated higher pressures and it was not until the balloon tyre appeared that lower pressures could be adopted.

£1 — £3

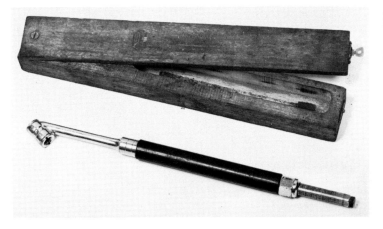

193. A Schrader's tyre gauge of a popular type
used in the 1920s and 1930s.
£1 — £3

194. Three further types of low pressure tyre gauges, note
variation of head. Note early types called 'Balloon Tyre
gauge'. 'Twenties and 'thirties.
£1 — £3

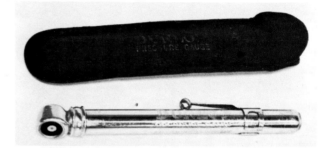

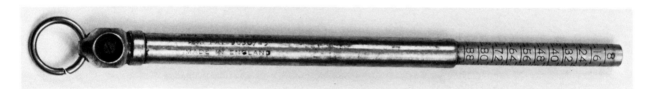

195. A high pressure tyre gauge, calibrated to 90lbs. 'Thirties.
£1 — £3

196. A useful tool, this Schrader valve key also embodies the ability to re-cut
internal and external threads on valve stems. Circa 1930.
£1 — £2

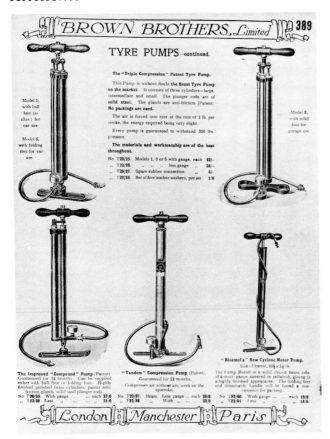

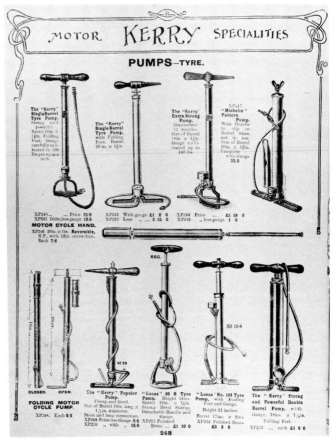

197. Tyre pumps in the form of hand or foot operated models. Shown here are variations from simple single cylinder to a triple compression type. These models all incorporate pressure gauges. Circa 1913.

198. A further selection of tyre pumps circa 1912, note variety available.

199. Two simple tyre pumps: left, steel bodied; right, brass bodied. 'Thirties.

£5 — £8 steel   £7 — £10 brass

200. Shown here with its original 'thirties catalogue, a Dunlop 'standard' foot pump, steel frame, brass cylinder.
£15 — £25

201. It is difficult to find the large garage pumps, circa 1913, which were soon replaced by compressors. Such models incorporate pressure gauges and were hand operated. Below left, the famous Wood-Milne foot pump and, right, a fascinating device.

202. Monsieur Bibendum, the famous Michelin man, seated astride a garage tyre compressor, electrically operated, length of tubing coming from mouth connected to compressor mounted on two wheels with support at front. Now becoming scarce. 1920s.

£80 — £100

203. From Brown Brothers' 1913 catalogue, two examples of beaded edge motor tyres, giving American and metric sizes, and prices.

356 **BROWN BROTHERS, Limited**

"MACINTOSH" MOTOR TYRES.

MINIMUM RETAIL PRICES.
(Price List, dated October, 1912.)

"Macintosh" Tyres are being supplied to the large taxicab companies with complete satisfaction. Some of them are using "Macintosh" Tyres exclusively; therefore no further proof will be wanted of their wearing properties, as it is obvious that these companies are compelled to use those tyres which in running prove to be the most economical.

Although "Macintosh" Tyres have not been given the publicity their merit warrants through the usual advertising channels, owing to the demand exceeding the rate of production, the manufacturers have now made large extensions in buildings and plant, and they are able to cater for a larger share of the trade.

The Patent Fibre Steel Studded Tyres are giving remarkably good mileage records. The complete tread is moulded to the casing under hydraulic pressure, and the studs are more firmly secured to the tread and freer from movement than is the case with any other make.

"MACINTOSH" MOTOR COVERS AND TUBES.
List No. T8/3. "Mackintosh" Motor Tyres.

Millimetre sizes.

Millimetres.	Grooved Cover or 3-ribbed. £ s. d.	Tube and Valve. £ s. d.	Steel Studded Cover. £ s. d.
650 } 65	2 1 10	0 12 3	—
700 } 65	2 4 8	0 12 9	—
750 } 65	2 6 7	0 13 11	—
800 } 65	2 9 1	0 14 9	—
700 } 80	2 7 5	0 13 11	—
750 } 80	2 10 2	0 14 9	—
800 } 80	2 12 9	0 15 7	—
700 } 85	2 17 3	0 16 8	—
750 } 85	3 0 10	0 17 6	—
800 } 85	3 4 5	0 18 11	—
700 } 90	3 17 0	1 0 10	4 4 5
760 } 90	4 2 6	1 1 11	4 10 10
810 } 90	4 5 3	1 3 7	4 17 3
870 } 90	4 13 9	1 5 7	5 5 3
910 } 90	4 18 0	1 6 8	5 10 10
760 } 100	5 8 8	1 5 8	6 1 6
810 } 100	5 17 2	1 7 4	6 10 5
870 } 100	6 7 2	1 9 0	7 0 1
910 } 100	6 13 3	1 10 11	7 7 7
775 } 105	5 9 8	1 6 8	6 2 6
815 } 105	5 18 2	1 8 4	6 11 5
875 } 105	6 6 10	1 10 0	7 1 1
915 } 105	6 14 3	1 11 11	7 8 7
820 } 120	7 0 9	1 13 1	7 5 10
850 } 120	7 7 4	1 13 11	7 12 3
880 } 120	7 12 9	1 15 10	7 19 2
920 } 120	8 0 2	1 17 6	8 6 4
895 } 135	8 13 2	2 0 3	9 4 5
935 } 135	9 2 10	2 3 1	9 15 3

American sizes.

Inches.	Grooved or 3-ribbed. £ s. d.	Steel Studded. £ s. d.	Tube and Valve. £ s. d.
28 × 3	2 12 0	—	0 16 6
30 × 3	2 15 0	—	0 17 6
30 × 3½	4 10 0	5 5 0	1 2 0
32 × 3½	4 15 0	5 12 6	1 4 0
34 × 3½	5 2 6	6 0 0	1 6 0
32 × 4	7 16 7	9 2 6	2 5 9
34 × 4	8 6 3	9 14 0	2 8 9
36 × 4	8 16 10	10 6 0	2 11 9
34 × 4½	10 11 2	12 7 6	3 0 0
36 × 5	13 13 9	16 1 9	3 9 0

London *Manchester* *Paris*

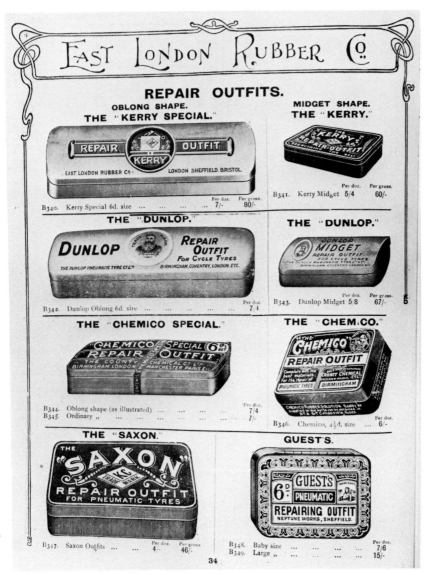

204. From an age when punctures were a frequent occurrence, every motorist had to be ready to repair his own tyres. A number of companies produced puncture repair outfits normally in colourful printed tins. The collector of tin boxes will be a competitor for these and similar items.

206. 'The Tyre Doctor' by Rubbermax included filler, emery cloth, and instruction sheet for repairs to cut tyres.
£3 — £5

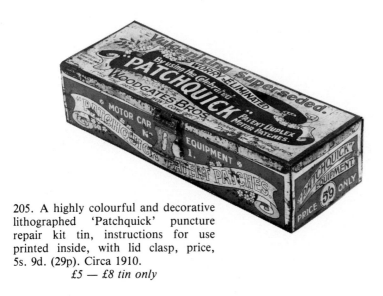

205. A highly colourful and decorative lithographed 'Patchquick' puncture repair kit tin, instructions for use printed inside, with lid clasp, price, 5s. 9d. (29p). Circa 1910.
£5 — £8 tin only

207. Used only on motorcycles in more recent years, security bolts were used on narrow section tyres to prevent creep. Also shown, further repair accessories.

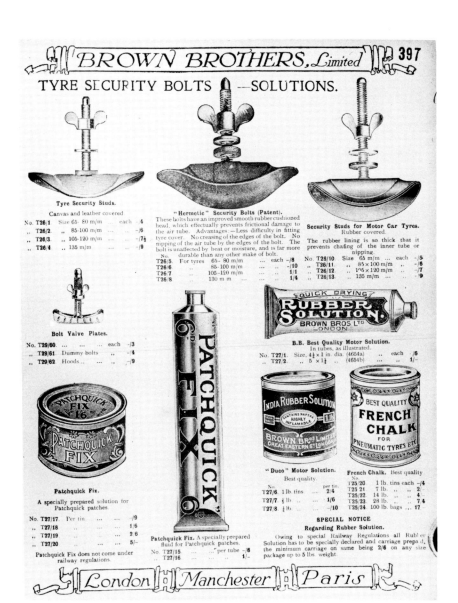

208. French chalk was a requirement when patches and solution were used for puncture repairs, as opposed to today's vulcanising, as it prevented the inner tube sticking to the cover. Dunlop produced this product in a decorative yellow and red tin flask with removable base. Mid-'thirties.

£1 — £2

209. The contents of a Chemico Motor repair kit, with special scissors, stamped patches, French chalk, etc. Late 1920s.

£3 — £5

210. The 'Magnalite' multi-purpose inspection lamp was ingenious in its electro-magnetic base which enabled it to be secured to any metal surface (except aluminium). This product was advertised in Riches catalogue of 1937 at a cost of 7s. 6d. (37½p) with bulb.

£8 — £12

211. A similar multi-purpose lamp to above, this time using a simple rubber suction pad to secure it to any smooth surface. The 'IVY' lamp here, shown with its original tin and label giving details, was also advertised in Riches catalogue of 1937, this time priced at 6s. 6d. (32½p).

£10 — £15

212. A 1930s inspection lamp with swivel head and clip, protective grip to bulb. This and the two previous lamps were supplied with a length of flex and two-pin plug to fit lighting switchboard (as present on some pre-war cars).

£5 — £8

213. Popular for some time, this Lucas brass bodied inspection lamp incorporates long extension flex enabling lamp to be used on almost any part of the car. When not in use the large hook doubles as winding handle for internal spool and stores cable neatly. Pre-war price 12s. 6d. (62½p); a carrying clip was obtainable for the additional outlay of 1s. (5p). Also encountered with painted finish and issued as standard equipment on military vehicles throughout World War II.

£5 — £8

214. A 'Stronlite' bulb container with provision for one head lamp bulb, a side light bulb and tail light bulb, in practical light aluminium case. Circa 1930.

£5 — £8

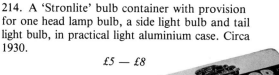

215. The contents of the Splendor 'Motor Lamp Outfit' tin have been removed, but it is still attractive for the collector, depicting early 'thirties car in black over orange. Below, a selection of pre-war motor lamp bulbs in original boxes.

£1.50 — £3 outfit tin
£5 — £10
bulbs in boxes, collection

216. A necessity for some pre-World War II vehicles, the Trembler coil was an alternative to magneto ignition. Normally presented in attractive polished mahogany cases as illustrated, single cylinder type, this item by F.R. Butt & Co., London. Circa 1910.

£20 — £40

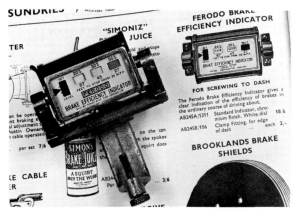

217. With patent dates for 1929, this Ferodo Brake Efficiency Indicator is fitted with additional dashboard clamp and shown here against original Riches catalogue for 1937. Colours indicate 'Fair' (red), 'Good' (yellow) and 'Very Good' (green). A useful and interesting accessory.

£25 — £35

218. The Ferodo Brake Efficiency Indicator pictured with an original manufacturer's leaflet, showing variation to efficiency percentages.

See 217 for price

219. A good quality Weston vehicle electrical equipment testing set, complete in fitted leather case with instruction book. 'Twenties.

£15 — £20

220. For use in determining head lamp power, this Auto-photometer incorporates its own ruler to calculate accurately distance from lamp, and operates in the same manner as a photographer's light meter. In its finger jointed mahogany case with instructions.

£20 — £30

221. A magneto spare parts outfit in mahogany case.
£15 — £20

222. With their original green leatherette box, a selection of colour samples produced by C.A. Willey Co., New York City, U.S.A. and bearing vendor's instructions. 1930s.

£5 — £8

223. Foreign oil and polish cans, with practical pourer on French oil can, centre. Left, French metal polish and, right, American car body polish.

£2 — £4 each

224. Valve grinding compound, dual compartmented tin, one side taking fine, the other coarse carborundum paste. 'Twenties and 'thirties.

£1 — £2

225. The possibility of a fire hazard encouraged the production of fire extinguishers to be carried in the vehicle. A typical brass bodied hand operated pump extinguisher by Pyrene, pre-war. Other manufacturers' similar products encountered.

£5 — £8

226. A refill can for use with a Minimax fire extinguisher. 'Thirties.

£1 — £2

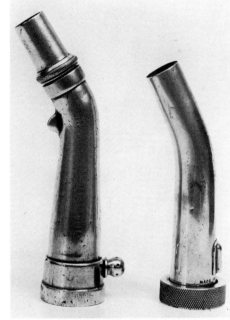

228. Two brass petrol can filler nozzles, a fine gauze filter is incorporated in design, with different types of vents to avoid air locks when pouring. Circa 1905-35.
£5 — £8 each

227. From the days when petrol was purchased in two gallon cans, nozzles were essential to avoid spillage. Left, filler with flexible extension which incorporates breather to prevent blow-back, and right, a filler of brass construction incorporating filter, key to slacken can filler cap and domed breather. 1920s.
£3 — £5 left
£5 — £8 right

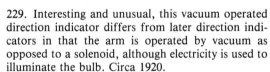

229. Interesting and unusual, this vacuum operated direction indicator differs from later direction indicators in that the arm is operated by vacuum as opposed to a solenoid, although electricity is used to illuminate the bulb. Circa 1920.
£15 — £20

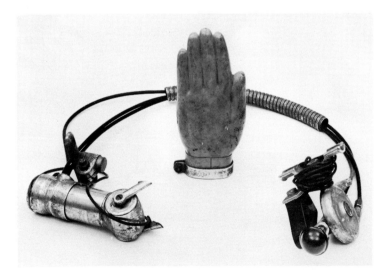

230. Operated by cable from the dash, this 'Birdglow' lifelike mechanical hand would represent driver's hand signals and was particularly effective after dark as the hollow hand was illuminated by a concealed bulb. English. Circa 1930.
£75 — £100

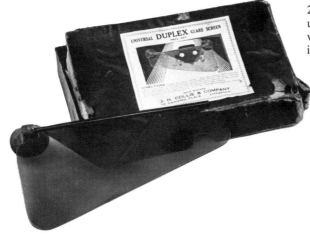

231. A useful anti-dazzle device, this Duplex universal glare screen had suction pad fixing to windscreen and is shown here with its original box indicating night use. 'Thirties.
£10 — £15

232. An inner/outer windscreen wiper, manually operated, inner rubber blade missing. Hand operated wipers were still in use as late as World War II on Jeeps. 'Twenties.
£12 — £18

233. Displaying a large 'H' to the centre of honeycomb, this nickel Hillman radiator dates from the mid-'twenties. 23ins.:58cm high.
£40 — £60

234. A fine nickel plated brass radiator from a Minerva, complete with its original enamelled badge, core sound, 29ins.:74cm high. Circa 1920.
£75 — £100

29. & 31. Gt Eastern St London.

CLOTHING SECTION.
WATERPROOF DRIVING APRONS.

SPECIAL **V** SHAPE FOR MOTOR DRIVING.

Two Pockets.   Straps to Fasten at Back.

MC62	"**Epsom**" superior Cloth to good Rubber Sheeting ... each	**39**·
MC63	"**Kempton**" best Cloth to good Rubber Sheeting ... each	**47**·
MC64	"**Newmarket**" best Check Wool Lining to best Rubber Sheeting each	**56**·

60 × 50 in. APRONS.
Made with "Turn-over Edges" and fitted with Nickel Mounts.

MC65	Serge Cloth to India Rubber Sheeting each	**17/6**
MC66	"**President**" Cloth to India Rubber Sheeting ... ... each	**24/-**
MC67	"**Derby**" Check Wool Cloth to superior India Rubber Sheeting each	**29**·
MC68	"**Wrexham**" Fancy Seal to superior India Rubber Sheeting ... each	**33/6**
MC69	"**Epsom**" superior "President" Cloth to good India Rubber Sheeting ... ... each	**37**·
MC70	"**Kempton**" best "President" Cloth to good India Rubber Sheeting ... ... each	**44/-**
MC71	"**Newmarket**" best Check Wool Lining to best India Rubber Sheeting ... ... each	**56/-**
MC72	"**Rex**" superior proofed Box Cloth to Fancy Check Wool Lining, each	**59/-**

WATERPROOF TRI-CAR APRONS.

Fitted with necessary Straps.
Affords complete protection from chest to feet.

Each

MC73	Serge Cloth to American Sheeting	**13 6**
MC74	Serge Cloth to India Rubber Sheeting	**15 6**
MC75	"President" Cloth to India Rubber Sheeting	**18/-**
MC76	"Derby" Cloth to best India Rubber Sheeting	**23**·

89

235. Note the apron providing waterproofing for driver's legs, very few of these will have survived the ravages of time. Advertised 1911.

236. As an alternative to leather, this woollen motorist coat is of double breasted style with windcheating double buttoning flap, and bears the label of Alfred Dunhill Ltd., Automobile Tailors. Fine condition. Circa 1910.
£60 — £90

Left: 237. Described as an undercoat, this leather garment had a special wind-cheating double flap buttoned front, and was for use beneath the usual motorcoat or waterproofs. See also 244, left.
£40 — £60

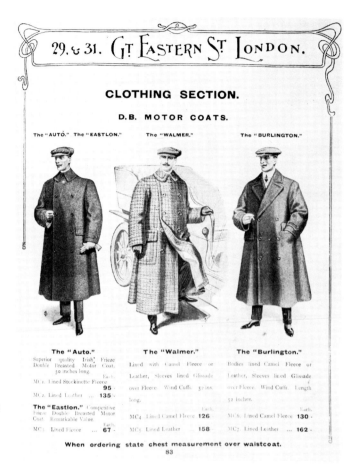

29. & 31. Gt. Eastern St. London.

CLOTHING SECTION.

D.B. MOTOR COATS.

The "AUTO." The "EASTLON." The "WALMER." The "BURLINGTON."

The "Auto."
Superior quality Irish Frieze Double Breasted Motor Coat, 50 inches long.
Each.
MC.1. Lined Stockinette Fleece **95** -
MC.2. Lined Leather ... **135** -

The "Eastlon." Competitive Frieze Double Breasted Motor Coat. Remarkable Value.
Each.
MC.3. Lined Fleece ... **67** -

The "Walmer."
Lined with Camel Fleece or Leather, Sleeves lined Glissade over Fleece. Wind Cuffs. 52 ins. long.
Each.
MC4. Lined Camel Fleece **126** -
MC5. Lined Leather ... **158** -

The "Burlington."
Bodies lined Camel Fleece or Leather, Sleeves lined Glissade over Fleece. Wind Cuffs. Length 52 inches.
Each.
MC6. Lined Camel Fleece **130** -
MC7. Lined Leather ... **162** -

When ordering state chest measurement over waistcoat.
83

Right: 238. Traditional heavy winter coats, normally available in double breasted style and a specific motorist accessory.
£00 — £00

239. Although technically a flying coat, the protection afforded by these leather garments appealed strongly to the motorist in the 'twenties, and many were sold as surplus to the R.A.F. following the introduction of the one piece Sidcot flying suit. Note large map pocket at breast, windproof cuffs, etc.
£120 — £180

240. Another flying/motoring leather coat, slight styling variation.
£80 — £100

241. A motorist's leather helmet of the type universally worn by motorists, motorcyclists and aviators. Circa 1914.
£15 — £20

242. A white leather motoring helmet with peak and rolled forward ear vent covers. Circa 1930.
£15 — £20

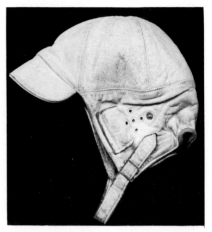

243. A slightly later catalogue also advertises the 'Dust Coat' (presumably a popular garment), and crash helmet intended for motorcyclists and aviators, but also worn by racing drivers.

244. This 1911 catalogue illustration also depicts a dust coat, a lightweight coat for summer wear intended to protect normal clothing from dust.

245. Protective goggles of the type favoured by early motorists. Left, leather semi-face mask, elasticated strap, removable hinged lenses. 'Limpida patent'. Circa 1910. Also shown, above, leather semi-face mask type goggles with elasticated back and laminated lenses. Circa 1913.
£10 — £15 each

246. A good pair of leather driving goggles shown with their leather case stamped Dunhill London. Circa 1920.
£12 — £18

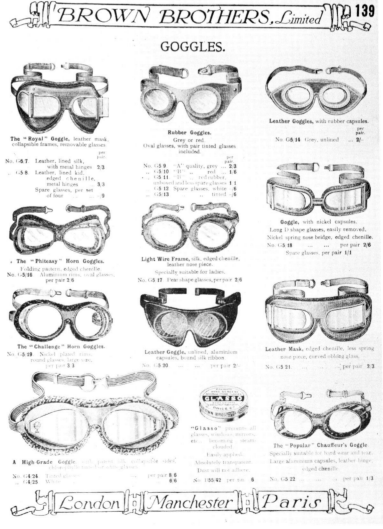

247. Protection for the eyes was provided by a variety of goggles, some idea of the range available illustrated here. Circa 1913.

248. A pair of Willson goggles, shown here with imitation tortoiseshell side protectors and frame, original case. Circa 1914.

£5 — £8

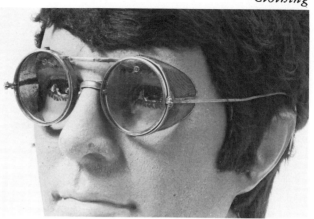

249. A pair of driving glasses or goggles with perforated side protectors. Circa 1914.

£5 — £8

250. Unusual tinted driving glasses employing side lenses. Circa 1914.

£7 — £10

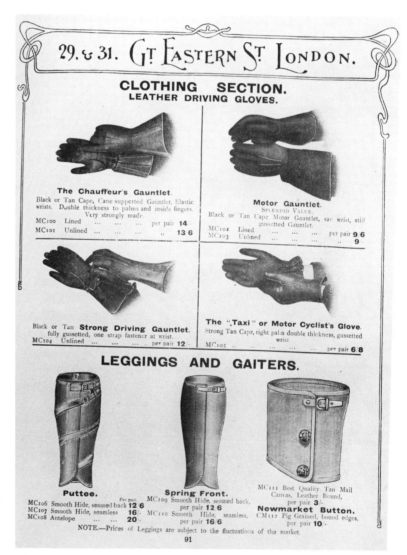

251. For use in the exposed open car, a catalogue selection of driving gloves and gauntlets. Also shown, leggings and gaiters, popular with some motorists.

344 BROWN BROTHERS, Limited

TRUNKS.

Brooks' Weatherproof Trunks for the Roof or Canopy.

Either singly, in pairs, or in sets of three, four or five etc., as required. In special strength and finish for the colonies and tropical climates.

Illustration shows a pair, and will give some idea of their handsome appearance, neatness of attachment, and size and capacity.

Made with square corners, the cost is much less than where they are shaped to the rail.

The trunks are securely held together by means of the Brooks' Patent Instantus Holders, and are attached to the rail by the finest quality stout leather straps provided with Brooks' Patent Tautum Buckles, a simple lever device ensuring absolute tautness of the straps, or they can be fixed to the roof itself by our patent holders.

List No.	Mfrs No.	FIRST QUALITY (Leather bound)	each £ s. d.	List No.	Mfrs No.	FIRST QUALITY (Leather bound)	each £ s. d.
T6/1	1417	24 × 20½ × 12 in.	£4 8 6	T6/6	1124	46 × 21½ × 12 in., with web straps and corners shaped to rail	£7 10 0
T6/2	1418	36 × 18 × 12 in., with 3 in. tray	5 6 6				
T6/3	1121	45 × 24½ × 12 in., square corners	6 5 0	T6/7	1125	48 × 20½ × 12 in., square corners	6 2 0
T6/4	1122	45 × 21½ × 12 in., with web straps and corners shaped to rail	7 12 6	T6/8	1126	48 × 20½ × 12 in., with web straps	6 7 6
						SECOND QUALITY.	
T6/5	1123	46 × 21½ × 12 in., square corners	6 1 6	T6/9	1127	48 × 20 × 12 in., square corners	5 6 0

Note.—Web straps, removable divisions, boot boxes, trays, or any other internal fittings, can be fitted to any of our standard roof trunks where specified

Brooks' Waterproof Grids. FIRST QUALITY.

List No.	Size	Manufacturer's No.	£ s. d.
T6/10	27 × 14 × 12 in.	525	each 4 2 0
T6/11	27 × 16 × 14 in.	1100	4 6 0
T6/12	30 × 14 × 12 in.	1101	4 5 0
T6/13	32 × 14 × 12 in.	1102	4 6 0
T6/14	32 × 18 × 14 in.	1103	4 12 6
T6/15	34 × 18 × 14 in.	1104	4 14 0
T6/16	36 × 14 × 12 in.	1105	4 9 0
T6/17	36 × 18 × 14 in.	1106	4 16 0

SECOND QUALITY.
(Possessing all the leading features of the first quality, but fewer refinements in details and finish.)

List No.	Size	Manufacturer's No.	£ s. d.
T6/18	27 × 14 × 12 in.	1107	each 3 8 0
T6/19	27 × 16 × 14 in.	1108	3 10 0
T6/20	34 × 18 × 14 in.	1111	3 18 0
T6/21	30 × 14 × 12 in.	1109	3 10 0
T6/22	32 × 14 × 12 in.	1110	3 11 0

Brooks' Waterproof Grid Trunks.

The Brooks' Patent Tool Cabinets. Attached to the Footboard by the Brooks' **Patent Instantus Holders.** Fitted with trays.

Cabinets complete with pair of Patent Instantus Holders.

List No.	Mfrs' No.		£ s. d.	Complete with Patent Holders. £ s. d.
T4/10	1134	10½ × 10½ × 8½ in. deep, 3 trays, length extended, 25½ in., finest polished solid oak	1 10 0	2 5 0
T4/11	1136	Ditto, ditto, best mahogany	1 12 6	2 7 6
T4/12	1135	Ditto, ditto, finest teak, Colonial finish	1 16 0	2 11 0
T4/13	1137	14 × 10½ × 10½ in. deep, 4 trays, length extended, 32 in., finest polished solid oak	1 16 0	2 11 0
T4/14	1139	Ditto, ditto, best mahogany	2 1 0	2 16 0
T4/15	1138	Ditto, ditto, finest teak, Colonial finish	2 3 0	2 18 0
T4/16	519	20 × 9 × 10½ in. deep, 3 trays, length extended, 20 in., finest polished solid oak	2 1 0	2 16 0
T4/17	1179	Ditto, ditto, best mahogany	2 5 0	3 0 0
T4/18	1178	Ditto, ditto, finest teak. Colonial finish	2 8 0	3 3 0

Brooks' Tool Cabinet.

London Manchester Paris

252. An attractive motor cushion bearing embroidered Bentley black label badge. 14¼ins.:36cm square. 'Thirties.
£15 — £25

253. Before the days of integral boots, roof racks were used to some extent to carry baggage, etc. Shown here purpose-made waterproofed trunks for the motorist. Centre illustration shows grid mounted trunk. Bottom, a running board mounted tool cabinet.

254. An Edwardian roof travelling trunk, note curved base to fit bowed roof, green leatherette covered. Circa 1910.
£15 — £25

255. For the lone traveller this high quality one man picnic set includes stove, collapsible cup, sandwich box, milk flask, etc. in its fitted leather case produced by Barrett & Sons, Piccadilly, London. Unusual as single outfit, normally for family use. Circa 1920.
£25 — £40

Colour Plate 3. An attractive and practical Hattersley & Davidson multi-stage foot pump which utilises three cylinders of varying diameter and incorporates pressure gauge. Finished in lacquered brass with black painted frame, red fittings. Circa 1915.

$£25 — £35$

Badges (Club and Other)

From the early days, the motor organisations issued badges of distinctive type to their members. These badges enabled instant identification of members' vehicles and were leased in return for a yearly fee. All manner of courtesy was extended to members; in addition to roadside assistance, patrolmen saluted members and advised of hazards. Almost at once, many clubs became affiliated to the R.A.C., incorporating their own device on R.A.C. associates' badges.

Other clubs were formed, either for competition, e.g. Brooklands Automobile Racing Club, or make clubs, e.g. M.G., Riley Owners', etc., these producing badges of their own designs, usually plated and enamelled.

The Brooklands Automobile Racing Club provided enamelled lapel badges suspended on cord for members and pin-backed brooches for guests. These are dated and many interesting designs are to be encountered.

256. A fine quality large size R.A.C. full member's car badge, this badge was approved by King Edward VII and first used in 1907 when the club received Royal patronage and became known as the Royal Automobile Club. The badge design consists of a crowned motor wheel centred by a bust of Edward VII and supported by the torso of Mercury. The reverse is centred with an enamelled Union Jack. A variation of this badge in similar form but with Queen's Crown is still issued to full members.

£120 — £180

257. The front and reverse of a scarce R.A.C. full member's badge with circular enamelled Union Jack. Circa 1912.

£60 — £80

258. An R.A.C. full member's small size badge with radiator cap mounting is shown here with cap, manufactured by Elkington & Co. Ltd. and intended to be displayed with the King's head facing forward. Reverse shows rectangular enamelled Union Jack and badge number C2707.

£40 — £60

259. Left, a cast R.A.C. full member's badge with badge bar or radiator cap mounting, Union Jack to reverse, 5¼ins.:13.5cm. Right, die struck small size full member's badge with radiator grille mounting, plain to reverse, 4ins.:10.5cm high.

£20 — £30 left
£15 — £25 right

260. A Royal Automobile Club scout's badge in brass, an accurate miniature of the full member's badge and having loops to reverse for use with pin. Pre-1920.

£8 — £12

261. For the associated R.A.C. member a different badge issued and introduced in 1908, having enamelled Union Jack to centre. The membership renewal disc is visible through spokes, the reverse would bear date and year of expiry, the associate member's number stamped to base. Nickel plated finish.

£35 — £50

262. A radiator type cap mounting of an R.A.C. associate member's badge, this time in brass, showing severe damage to enamelling, renewal card missing.

£15 — £20

263. Another R.A.C. associate's badge, a later and smaller version. A re-finished example, the wings of Mercury do not extend beyond arms, indicating a later pattern. By this time brass had been replaced by a white metal alloy which was a poorer base for plating and became brittle with age, shown on bar mounting, and would have been positioned on bar support between front wings. The enamelled centre is mounted improperly. In 1936 this Union Jack centre was replaced by the R.A.C. monogram enamelled white on blue field.

£15 — £25

264. A light car size 1908 pattern R.A.C. associate member badge which could also be used on motorcycles, 2¾ins.:6.75cm diameter. Shown here with reverse with blue year disc for 1927, motorcycle version had red disc.

£20 — £30

265. A 1908 pattern Royal Automobile Club associate's brass badge with enamelled Union Jack, annual renewal disc just visible through spokes, bracket intended for scuttle mounting.

£20 — £30 enamel damaged

266. A 1908 pattern R.A.C. associate member's badge, here official centre with device of the Dorset Automobile Club founded in 1904. Under terms of membership members of associated clubs were entitled to incorporate their own Club device. Renewal disc visible.

£50 — £75

268. Here shown with bumper bracket base, this R.A.C. associate's badge is chromium plated over base metal and has Union Jack enamelled centre, 3¾ins.:9.5cm high. Circa 1930-35.

£15 — £25

267. Above, introduced in 1908 and normally found with Union Jack enamelled centre, this R.A.C. associate's badge displays centre of Cheshire Automobile Club. Other associated club centres are to be found, and are illustrated in early members' handbooks. The Cheshire Automobile Club was formed in February, 1907. Right, a post-1908 R.A.C. associate member's badge with central enamelled device of the North Eastern Automobile Association (established 1904), showing member's renewal ticket in white celluloid, c.1910.

£50 — £75 each

269. In 1936 the R.A.C. associate's badge was altered to incorporate the R.A.C. associate insignia, thus replacing Union Jack, see previous illustration. Plated finish, enamelled centre.

£12 — £18

270. A first pattern Automobile Association member's badge introduced in 1906; note impressed signature 'Stenson Cooke', the association's first secretary. This style of badge with signature was used until the amalgamation with the Motor Union, and in 1911 the two organisations produced a combined badge. Available in nickel, brass or steel.

£75 — £100

271. With the amalgamation, a new badge was designed incorporating the outline and winged wheel motif of the Motor Union, large and medium sized versions shown here. The suffix letter at end of numerals indicates later issue. Large size 6½ins.:16.5cm high, medium size 5ins.:12.5cm high.

£25 — £40 large   £15 — £25 medium

272. Emphasising the ownership of the badge, this version is stamped with address and instructions of the Automobile Association, reverse side shown. For a short period during World War I, small enamelled heart-shaped inserts were issued to affix to badge immediately under winged wheel to prove renewal of membership. These are scarce. One of the authors has encountered three with maroon hearts (expiring 1916) and one blue (1915). An earlier yellow is also thought to exist.

£10 — £15

274. Post-war, the A.A. badge adopted a raised convex form using yellow backing. Two examples shown, slight variations.

£5 — £8

273. A light car (small) size A.A. member's badge, 4½ins.:11.5cm high. As with 264, a version stamped 'Cycle' exists for use on motorcycles. Solid nickel, 1920s.

£20 — £30

275. Automobile Association members' keys providing access to roadside telephones. Shown here right, attractive fretted 1920 pattern, reverse with slogan 'The Key to the Open Road', and left, 1930s' issue (both fitted same lock).

£5 — £8 right   £1 — £2 left

276. A scarce A.A. patrolman's brass cap or collar badge. Circa 1920. *£5 — £8*

278. A good quality, well-enamelled 'Order of the Road' member's car badge. 'Thirties.
£10 — £15

277. Note the 'Member not Driving' cover with this Order of the Road enamelled member's badge and also date plaque for 1928-31. It is unusual to find these two items on surviving badges.
£20 — £30

280. Of World War I interest, this nickel National Motor Volunteers' badge featured a running Mercury; people displaying such a badge indicated their willingness for service on the home front. Circa 1914.
£40 — £60

279. Employing a military General Service badge superimposed on eight spoked wheel, this type of badge was carried on vehicles subsidised by the War Department and could be requisitioned in time of need. Brass, circa 1914.
£50 — £75

281. An impressive reminder of the days of Empire, this nickel plated Automobile Association of Bengal member's badge incorporates snarling tiger, radiator cap type mounting. 'Twenties.
£25 — £40

282. The Royal East African Automobile Association produced this chromium plated brass member's badge with prowling lion, note winged wheel motif. 4¾ins.:12cm high, circa 1940.
£5 — £10

283. An American Automobile Association California State plate for fixing to number plate.

£5 — £8

284. A cast Junior Car Club member's badge, aluminium with red and white enamelling. The Junior Car Club was responsible for organising many pre-war events at Brooklands. Post-war, with the demise of Brooklands, the J.C.C. became part of B.A.R.C.

£25 — £40

285. The famous Brooklands racing track opened July 6th 1907. Shown here a most colourful and attractive Brooklands Automobile Racing Club member's car badge, highly sought after, dramatically depicting the banking at the track. Examples exist with 120 m.p.h. and 130 m.p.h. tablets, indicating member's achievement of lap speeds exceeding 120 or 130 m.p.h. Records indicate that only thirteen qualified for the 130 m.p.h. badge and eighty-four for the 120 m.p.h. badge.
£75 — £125

286. Revived in 1930, the Brooklands Aero Club produced this badge of similar outline to the Car Club badge but incorporating aeroplane banking right. The new badges were offered through the 1932 year book at a cost of £1 (loan charge).
£75 — £125

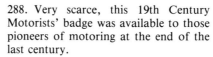

288. Very scarce, this 19th Century Motorists' badge was available to those pioneers of motoring at the end of the last century.

£100 — £150

287. A B.A.R.C. (British Automobile Racing Club) member's badge enamelled in blue, red, yellow and white, circa 1950 to present day.

£5 — £8

289. An attractive Italian Royal Automobile Club member's badge, with enamelled red, white, blue and black crest on alloy 'cog' backing. 5ins.:12.5cm high, circa 1930.

£15 — £25

Left: 290. Die struck and enamelled and retaining traces of nickel plating, a Spanish Royal Automobile Club badge in red, yellow and white. 'Thirties.

£5 — £8

Right: 291. Utilising 'cog' design, a French Automobile Club badge, chromium plated with raised red enamel lettering to centre and blue enamel to edge. 4¼ins.:11cm high, circa 1930.

£15 — £25

293. Shown with matching pennant, a Third Reich period enamelled club badge of The German Automobile Club, 3¼ins.:8cm wide. Circa 1935.
£25 — £40 pennant
£30 — £50 badge

294. Using 'made-up' backing to enable badge to be mounted on bar, a German Nürburg-Ring club badge enamelled in black, green and white. 'Forties.
£10 — £15

292. Incorporating steering wheel in design together with edelweiss, oak and laurel sprays, and national emblem in red and white enamel, a Swiss Touring Club badge, on badge bar bracket, chromium plated. 4¼ins.:11cm high, 'thirties.

£10 — £15

Left: 295. Interesting, in that it incorporates a jerboa (desert rat), an Ahmadi Desert Motoring Club badge. 'Forties.
£7 — £10

Right: 296. Incorporating a St. Christopher, a Vintage Sports Car Club badge, blue enamel, plated background. Post-war.

£7 — £10

297. Though the Latin translation is open to scholarly debate, 'Per Ardua ad Astra' was adopted by the Royal Flying Corps in March 1913. This brass R.A.F. car badge has enamelled centre and is of four piece construction. Circa 1930.
£12 — £18

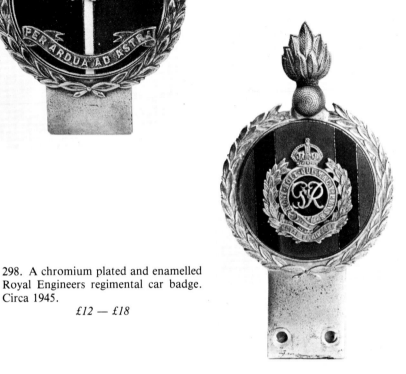

298. A chromium plated and enamelled Royal Engineers regimental car badge. Circa 1945.
£12 — £18

299. One of a series of badges of famous regiments, a Royal Marines car badge, chromium plated with St. Christopher and regimental badge, backing to badge in blue, red, green and yellow enamel. 3ins.:7.5cm wide. Post-war.
£12 — £18

Left: 300. Employing winged wheel similar to Austin emblem, this Civil Service Motoring Association badge has enamelled King's Crown. Chromium plated over brass. 3¾ins.:9.5cm wide. 'Forties.
£5 — £8

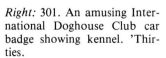

Right: 301. An amusing International Doghouse Club car badge showing kennel. 'Thirties.
£5 — £8

303. Produced for an owners club, this 'AC' Owners' Club badge is enamelled in white and blue, of particular interest and sought after by AC owners.
£12 — £18

302. Impressive with its high relief centre motif in the form of a buffalo's head, this Royal Antedeluvian Order of Buffaloes member's badge has blue enamel outer ring. Circa late 'thirties.
£8 — £10

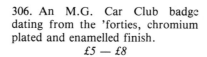

304. Taking its design from a 'knock-off' hub cap, a Bentley Drivers' Club badge, chrome and enamel. 'Forties.
£5 — £8

306. An M.G. Car Club badge dating from the 'forties, chromium plated and enamelled finish.
£5 — £8

305. Using the horseshoe radiator motif, a Bugatti Owners' Club badge, chrome with red enamel. 'Forties.
£5 — £8

307. Incorporating air cooled cylinders in motif, an interesting Southern Cross Motor Club car badge, c.1920.
£20 — £30

308. Rally plaques come in many forms. Shown here one relief, one enamelled finish. 'Thirties.
£2 — £5

309. A selection of post-war rally plaques, note Monte Carlo, Scottish Rally, Tulip Rally, etc. Late 'forties, early 'fifties.
£2 — £5

310. Left, an Amilcar enamelled radiator badge from the 1920s. During this period most manufacturers produced radiator badges for their cars. On the right, a UNIC enamelled radiator badge, again from the 'twenties.
£5 — £8 Amilcar
£5 — £8 UNIC

311. An early Brooklands guest's brooch with pin back, issued 1911.
£8 — £12

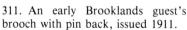

312. Red and white enamel suspended guest's brooch for Brooklands 1926. Note similarity to member's badge in 314.
£8 — £12

313. Brooklands members' lapel badges, various year designs, enamel finish, here shown with original suspension cords. 1920-38.

£8 — £12 each

314. Further Brooklands badges, including late 'thirties racing car shape. These badges were numbered on reverse side and were issued in a cardboard box together with two guests' brooches.

£8 — £12 each

315. An original box to contain Brooklands badges (one member's badge and two guests' brooches) giving free entry to course, detail to lid. 1936.

316. Immediately after the war, the Brooklands Automobile Racing Club became part of the Junior Car Club and in 1948 the first motor race was held at Goodwood. In January 1949 the initials B.A.R.C. were again used, this time as the British Automobile Racing Club. The two larger badges are early 'fifties members' badges, again with enamel finish and numbered backs. Also shown, the guests' brooches (smaller) for the members' badges in similar two-tone enamel finish.

£3 — £5 each

317. On the left, a good quality gilt and blue enamelled R.A.C. 'Committee' lapel badge. 2ins:5cm high. Circa 1920. On the right, an attractive Edwardian hallmarked silver and enamelled Motor Union badge, c.1907.

£10 — £15 R.A.C.
£10 — £15 M.U.

318. A selection of lapel badges including, top: Texaco, Order of the Road, Dennis; centre: Paige Jewett Cars, Automobile Club of Great Britain and Ireland; bottom: AEC, Junior Car Club, Leyland.

£2 — £5 each

319. A further selection of lapel badges and brooches, including, top: The Society of Motor Manufacturers and Traders (committee member's badge for 3rd International Motor Exhibition), International Motor Exhibition, London 1949, Yorkshire Automobile Club 1905 (this club founded in January 1900). Below: Ulster Automobile Club badge, Nottinghamshire Automobile Club (founded 1900).

£3 — £6 each

320. A pre-war enamelled dealer's lapel badge, produced for Hartley & Midgley of Brighton as Ford main dealers, and an enamelled garage lapel badge for Caffyns Ltd.

£2 — £3

321. This dashboard 'St. Christopher' supplier's plate was undoubtedly sponsored by Shell. Finished in blue and white enamel, 1930s.

£3 — £5

322. St. Christopher, the patron saint of travellers, has been a popular subject for motorist key ring medallions or talismans. Shown here are examples produced for dashboard mounting. Pre-war.

£3 — £5

323. By a leading early 20th century silversmith, Omar Ramsden, this fine silver and enamel St. Christopher with five inset diamonds, was produced for dashboard mounting. 3¼ins.: 8cm wide, contained in original fitted case. Hallmarks for London, 1932, lovely item, probably sold by Liberty.

£550 — £750

324. A Leyland Motors by Appointment plate, pressed brass with enamelled shield and lower panel, Royal Crown missing from top of badge. 'Thirties.

£10 — £15

Mascots

Possibly the most collected of the motoring items are mascots, which originated as 'talismans' and developed into makers' mascots and accessory mascots, the quality of which may vary considerably from high sculptural to simple stylised products. A variety of finishes will be encountered from painted metal, bronze, brass, nickel, nickel plate, chromium plate, silver plate, gold plate or even glass.

Collectors have a wide choice and may prefer to specialise in makers' mascots, animal mascots or glass mascots to name but three areas.

Apart from the Lalique glass products, makers' mascots will probably be more expensive than accessory types, though in this area many clever novelty mascots exist — for instance Policeman with moving arms. Also in this section are Motor Meters (radiator cap temperature gauges), some of which incorporate mascot-like features and were sold in early catalogues as mascots. Post-war safety regulations have almost entirely outlawed the radiator mounted mascot.

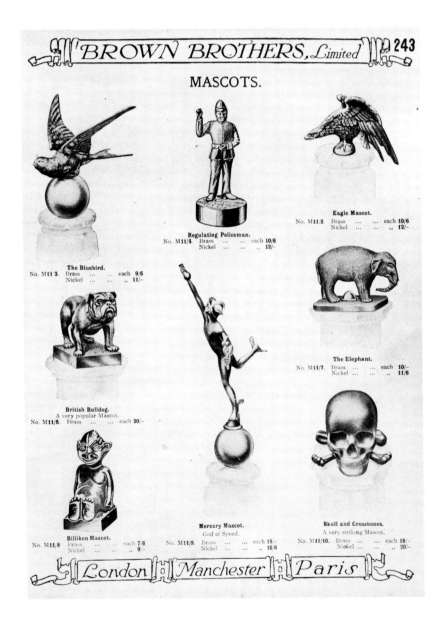

325. A page from the 1913 Brown Brothers Catalogue, illustrating accessory mascots available in either brass or nickel, an imaginative selection from primitive to classical.

326. Probably the most famous of all car mascots, the 'Spirit of Ecstasy' was conceived by the sculptor Charles Sykes in 1911 and can be found in bronze, nickel, chromium, etc. and in various sizes. Early mascots bear the full Charles Sykes signature together with patent date February 6th, 1911; later mascots use the abbreviation C. Sykes and R.R. Ltd. Shown here, a 7ins.:18cm Rolls-Royce Spirit of Ecstasy mascot bearing the full Charles Sykes signature and patent date and details, probably from a Silver Ghost, nickel plated. Circa 1920.

£150 — £180

327. With the introduction of the Rolls-Royce Twenty in 1922 a smaller mascot was produced. Shown here, a 5ins.: 13cm figure, again nickel plated, fully signed with patent date and details. Circa 1922.

£60 — £90

328. From the early 'thirties, signed C. Sykes, chromium plated and probably from a Phantom II, this mascot is 6½ins:16.5cm high and mounted on its radiator cap on a display plinth. The hexagon to radiator cap is an aid to removal.

£75 — £100

329. Introduced in the mid-'thirties, the 'Kneeling Lady' was also designed by Charles Sykes, normally signed C. Sykes, 26.1.34 and stamped 'US Pat. Off.' and 'Trade Mark reg.' 3½ins.:9cm high.
£60 — £90

330. A unique motoring item, this 'Wraith' plaque came from a 1910 40/50 Rolls-Royce, the owner later agreeing to allow Rolls-Royce to name a new model with this name in 1938. From a period when people sometimes named cars just as they did boats. Surmounted with large size 'Spirit of Ecstasy', silver plated and enamelled on ebony base.
£500 — £600

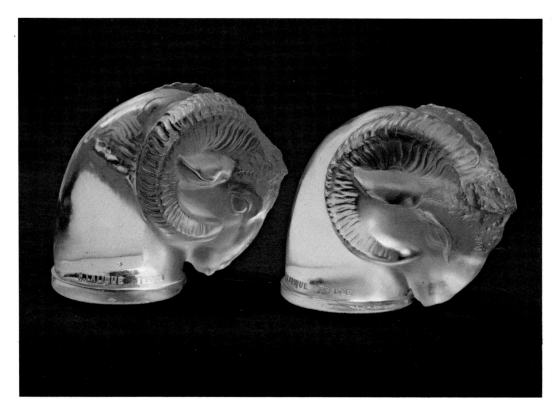

Colour Plate 4. Two Lalique glass rams' heads car mascots. See also no. 435 on p. 129.

Colour Plate 5. Three views of John Hassall's 'Robert' policeman mascot, silver plated brass, porcelain 'egg shaped' head. Circa 1920. See also no. 380, p. 115.

331. Another example from a 25/30 Rolls-Royce, this kneeling lady has good detail, traces of 'U.S. Pat. Office Reg' just visible inside wing, chromium plate, mounted on radiator cap. 1930s.
£60 — £90

332. Note pressure cap to base on this chromium plated Spirit of Ecstasy mascot from a late 20/25 Rolls-Royce. 1930s.

£75 — £100

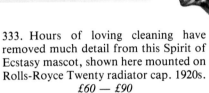

333. Hours of loving cleaning have removed much detail from this Spirit of Ecstasy mascot, shown here mounted on Rolls-Royce Twenty radiator cap. 1920s.
£60 — £90

Left: 334. A good dancing nymph car mascot with outstretched arms and flowing gown, brass. 5½ins.:14cm high. Pre-1920.

£40 — £60

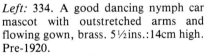

Right: 335. A winged sphinx mascot, possibly from a Rolland Pilain, plated brass, here shown mounted on turned wooden base. 5¼ins.:13.5cm high. Circa 1930.

£30 — £45

336. Large attractive accessory mascot in the form of cherub seated on winged wheel and playing a lyre, silver plated. Circa 1912. 7ins.:18cm high.
£60 — £80

´338. The mythological figure of Icarus was adopted by Farman cars through the company's association as an aircraft manufacturer. Although a French concern, this mascot was made by Finnigans, London. Circa 1925.
£180 — £250

337. This star shaped mascot with dancing nymph was the mascot of Star cars. Nickel plated brass, 3¾ins.:9.5cm high. Mid-1920s.
£35 — £50

339. Again of the Icarus theme, but probably for limited commercial sale, this mascot signed by Gordon Crosby, a famous motoring artist, dates from the late 1920s. Compare the modified style with previous illustrations. 5¾ins.: 14.5cm high. This mascot sold by Sotheby's Belgravia, October 1980, for £800.

340. This unusual winged mascot is centred by a figure of a naked nymph. The base is marked 'Theo Co. Ltd. L'pool.' Nickel plated. 10ins.:25.5cm wide.
£40 — £60

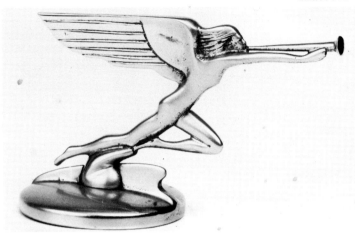

Above left: 341. A stylised Egyptian Goddess mascot, chromium plated on radiator cap. 1930s.

£20 — £30

Above right: 342. Bearing a striking similarity to Packard's Goddess of Speed, this trumpeter mascot is chromium plated and mounted on radiator cap.

£35 — £50

Left: 343. An attractive chromium plated brass nymph with shooting star signed J. Garnier. 5½ins.:14cm high, mounted on radiator cap and wooden base. Circa 1930.

£60 — £80

Right: 345. A small Vulcan mascot for Vulcan cars, plain circular base, nickel. 3¾ins.:9.5cm high, 1920s.
£35 — £50

344. Available in two different sizes and produced in brass and nickel, the figure of the god Vulcan stands beside anvil, leaning on hammer with hand holding wheel, used as standard on Vulcan vehicles. 3¼ins.:9cm high, circa 1920.
£35 — £50

Left: 346. From the same manufacturer, this Vulcan mascot has been silver plated, possibly for use as ornament. Integral cap. 6½ins.:16.5cm.
£45 — £60

347. Shown here with radiator cap, this winged female kneeling on winged wheel is a good quality accessory product, chromium plated. 1930s. 6¾ins.:17cm high.

£40 — £60

348. A Triumph Dolomite winged nymph mascot standing on globe, plated brass. 5¼ins.:13cm high, late 1930s.

£25 — £40

349. Wearing winged helmet and sandals, a running figure of Mercury, plated brass. 7ins.: 18cm high, circa 1930.

£35 — £40

350. Left to right: a popular 'Speed Nymph' accessory mascot on radiator cap mounting, 5ins.:12.5cm high, circa 1930; a Minerva 'Goddess Head' chrome-plated mascot circa 1930 (this mascot was a prize winning design in the 1921 Salon de L'Automobile mascot competition), 5ins.:12.5cm high; and a Cubitts 'Cupid' brass mascot on radiator cap mounting, signed and registered, 5¼ins.:13cm high, circa 1911.

£15 — £25 nymph   £60 — £90 Minerva   £40 — £60 Cupid

351. Used by Buick cars, a goddess figure conveying impression of speed. Chrome plated brass, 6¼ins.:16cm long, circa 1930.

£30 — £50

352. Signed F. Bazin, this bronze 'Shivering Fairy' mascot depicts figure standing on one leg with arms folded, note particularly the styled butterfly wings to back, which can be compared with Bazin's butterfly mascot illustrated on page 41 of *Car Mascots* by Signano & Sulzberger. Early 1920s.

£40 — £60

353. Dating from the 1920s, the 'Spirit of Triumph' a stylised male figure holding a wheel, this popular mascot was designed by the Frenchman, Bazin.
£50 — £75

354. With feet resting on winged wheel, a speed nymph of a style popular prior to World War II, 7ins.: 18cm high.

£40 — £60

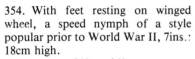

355. A 1930s speed nymph, one of the more common mascots of the period, available in various sizes and finishes. 4¼ins.:11cm high.
£15 — £25

356. Compare with previous 'popular' speed nymph, a bronzed brass example with longer flowing hair. 7ins.:17.5cm high.

£20 — £30

357. Described as 'Poise' when advertised in motor catalogues, this speed nymph mascot has arms outstretched behind and flowing drapery, plated brass, mid- to late 1930s. Note, original cost in 1934 £1. 1s. 0d. (£1.05).
£15 — £25

358. Leaning into the wind, this naked nymph mascot has contemporary bobbed hairstyle. Plated brass, circa 1930.

£15 — £25

359. A fine example of a Centaur archer used by Unic as their company mascot. Circa 1930.

£100 — £150

360. A cast bronze art deco style mascot in the form of a winged female figure, possibly Victory. 7¼ins.:18.5cm high, circa 1930.

£55 — £75

361. Again of art deco influence, this winged head mascot is of cast bronze, unusual. Circa 1930.

£40 — £60

362. Carrying the Victor's laurel wreath, a Grecian youth mascot, 7ins.:18cm high. 1930s.

£40 — £60

363. Mounted on non-original radiator cap, a Pegasus mascot adopted by Amilcar. Post-war, Desmo produced a Pegasus mascot, popular with ex-paratroopers, as the winged horse was the parachute regiment's adopted emblem in World War II.

£40 — £60

MASCOTS—continued.

Automatic Policeman Mascot.
The forward movement of the car causes the
arms to move up and down and propeller
to revolve.
No. M11/17. Aluminium ... each 15/-
Enamelled ... „ 16/6

The Friendly Policeman.
No. M11/18. Brass, oxidised
finish ... each 10/6

Swastika.
The Lucky Mascot.
Brass or nickel plated.
No. M11/20 Medium size... ... each 4/-
„ M11/41 Large ... ... „ 5/6

The British Lion Mascot.
Best workmanship and high grade finish.
No. M11/21. Brass ... each 18/-
Nickel plated „ 20/-

Lincoln Imp Mascot.
No. M11/22. Brass ... each 10/6
Nickel plated „ 12/6

Golden Eagle Mascot.
No. M11/25. Brass ... each 14/6
Nickel plated „ 16/-

Kangaroo Mascot.
No. M11/23 Brass ...each 17/6
Nickel plated „ 19/-

Billiken Twins Mascot.
No. M11/24. Brass ... each 10/-

The Griffin.
No. M11/19. Brass ... ... each 7/6
Nickel ... ... „ 8/6

'BROWN BROTHERS, Limited 245

London Manchester Paris

364. A further selection of accessory mascots. Certainly policemen would appear to have been popular
subjects. Note the 'automatic' model and also the swastika, then a symbol of good fortune before its
adoption by the Nazi party in 1923.

365. A scarce Willy's knight mascot of a half figure of armoured knight with lance, and turreted base forming radiator cap. Nickel plated (lance not original). 1920s.

£50 — £75

366. The London firm of Finnigans produced a variety of mascots, including this 'Dutch Boy' in brass. 6¼ins.:16cm high. 1920s.

£30 — £50

367. A prize winning mascot at the Salon de L'Auto in Paris 1921, depicts a jester seated on winged wheel signed P. de Soete, and known as 'La Folie de la Vitesse'. Mounted on onyx base, 8¼ins.: 21cm high overall, scarce and desirable.

£100 — £150

368. An attractive mascot in the form of a Highlander, base marked 'PHINEAS MASCOT OF THE U.C.L. and U.C.H.'. 6¼ins.:16cm high, 1920s.

£50 — £80

369. The Patron Saint of Travellers, St. Christopher, would have obvious demand as an accessory mascot. This model from the lower end of market, plated base metal. 5¾ins.:14.5cm high. Circa 1930.

£15 — £20

370. Sold as an accessory mascot, obviously with Lincoln owners in mind, possibly to replace or supplement the 'Greyhound' mascot, this plated statuette of Abraham Lincoln bears the date 1927, 6ins.:15cm high.

£60 — £100

371. Retailed by Gieves, the famous naval outfitters, this quality silver plated mascot is in the unmistakable form of a standing Lord Nelson with coiled rope behind. 6¾ins.:17cm high with base. 1930s.

£40 — £60

372. An unusual early mascot in the form of a naked young woman with flowing cloak around her shoulders, heavy silver plated finish on radiator cap mounting. 7½ins.:19cm high.

£20 — £30

373. The Pathfinder, a Red Indian chief mascot by Regno, plated. 3½ins.:9cm high, mounted on square plinth. Mid-1920s.

£40 — £60

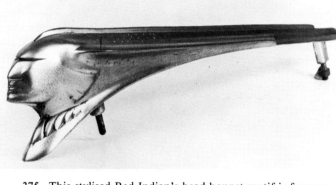

374. Wielding a tomahawk, a redskin car mascot, stylised and visually exciting. 1930s.

£40 — £60

375. This stylised Red Indian's head bonnet motif is from an immediate post-war Pontiac. Chromium plated, 17ins.:43cm long.

£10 — £15

376. Of the type of item produced from captured enemy aircraft metal and sold off to raise funds, this Churchill mascot incorporates the famous 'V' for Victory. Polished alloy. Circa 1945.

£30 — £50

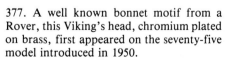

377. A well known bonnet motif from a Rover, this Viking's head, chromium plated on brass, first appeared on the seventy-five model introduced in 1950.

£2 — £5

244 **'BROWN BROTHERS, Limited'**

MASCOTS – continued.

The Swan.

No. M11/11. Brass ... ... each 10/6
Nickel ... ... ,, 12/-

Saint George and the Dragon.
A beautifully designed and finished mascot.

No. M11/12. Brass ... ... each 21/-
Nickel ... ... , 22/6

The Stag's Head.

No. M11/13. Brass ... ... each 7/6
Nickel ... ... ,, 9/-

Ally Sloper.
An exceedingly quaint Mascot.

No. M11/14. Brass ... ... each 24/-
Nickel ... ... ,, 26/-

Our "Empire" Mascot.
Beautifully designed and handsomely finished

No. M11/15. Polished brass... each 21/-
Nickel plated ... ,, 25/-
Silver ,, ... ,, 30/-

The Grinning Cat.

No. M11 16. Brass ... ... each 16/-
Nickel ... ... ,, 17/6

London *Manchester* *Paris*

378. The star of this page of accessory mascots is the 'Empire' mascot featuring Britannia and available in polished brass, nickel plated or silver plated. Another patriotic model is the one shown above, St. George and the Dragon. 1913. By 1923 the 'Empire' mascot had been renamed the 'King's' mascot and, for the inflation conscious, nickel plated models cost 40s. (£2).

379. Three amusing caricature mascots in bronze, each wearing fur coat, goggles and cap, one with a large motorhorn. Produced by Jean Verschneider, French, second decade twentieth century.

£80 — £120 each

380. The 'Robert', one of the most entertaining and amusing mascots, here shown in various poses with different facial expressions. The mascot was designed by John Hassall (1868-1948), and bears his name. The body and helmet are silver plated brass, the head of porcelain with painted features. 4½ins.:11.5cm high, 5¾ins.:14.5cm high on radiator cap base. Circa 1920. (See also Colour Plate 5, p. 104.)

£100 — £150 more common than the companion Aviator

381. An amusing Policeman mascot with a propeller which causes his arms to rise and fall in entertaining fashion, aluminium. Circa 1913.

£60 — £90

382. The previous mascot shown against an original catalogue advertisement and described as 'Automatic Policeman Mascot'. Available in aluminium at 15s. (75p) or enamelled at 16s. 6d. (82½p).

383. Halt! the Bobby, another version of this popular accessory mascot theme, here shown a stubby character, plated. 1920s. Note the description of 'Bobby' from a 1923 E.L.R. Co. motor catalogue: 'A delightfully irresponsible little mascot that will give joy and piquancy to the bonnet of the runabout 2-seater. It's quite impossible not to catch the cheery infection of this good-humoured caricature — even in the face of a bad puncture on the open road at night.' Original cost, height 5ins. £2. 17s. 6d. (£2.87½); 3ins. 16s. (80p). It must have been a good seller, particularly the 3ins. model, though that may have been difficult to see at night.

£25 — £40

384. One of the most popular mascots generally available was Bruce Bairnsfather's character 'Old Bill', a jovial moustachioed 'Tommy' wearing a scarf, and popularised by *The Bystander's* 'Fragments from France' produced during World War I. The mascot introduced shortly afterwards usually encountered in bronze or brass. Shown here a mascot and magazine depicting one of the famous Bairnsfather cartoons on cover.

£50 — £75 beware of recent copies

385. Another popular character of the 1920s was 'Burlington Bertie', here shown wearing leather helmet, holding monocle to eye and carrying fuel can inscribed 'Juice'. A scarce mascot and obviously desirable.

£80 — £120

386. The popularity of Chaplin's comic 'Little Tramp' is captured here as a car mascot in characteristic pose. 5½ins.:14cm high. 1930s.

£80 — £120

387. Popularised by a song 'Dinkie Doo', a cupid-like figure standing holding a bow (damaged). Brass, 5¼ins.:13.5cm high. Circa 1920s.

£20 — £30

388. Usually sold as a radiator mascot, this amusing drinking figure seated astride a barrel is the mascot of the Ancient Order of Froth Blowers. Seen here mounted as ashtray, silver plated. 1930s.

£30 — £50

244 MASCOTS MASCOTS

EAGLE MASCOT

Futurist design. Chromium plated Finish. Overall length, 6¾".
AM34A/1509 (1058) ... ... each **21/-**

Small Model. Overall length, 4¾".
AM34B/905 (1059) ... ... each **12/6**

SWALLOW MASCOT

AM37A/1809 Oxydized Silver Plate
Finish (1123)... each **25/-**
AM37B/2008 All Chromium Finish
(C1123) each **27/6**
N.B.—Supplied with Standard or Radiator Thermometer Fitting.

"GOLFING" MASCOT
(MM477)

Chromium Plated Finish. Height, 5½".
AM40A/2802 ... ... each **37/6**

MIGRATION MASCOT
(MM487)

Chromium finish. 5¼" length. 2½" high. Futurist design.
AM35D/1103 ... ... each **15/-**

STADIUM MASCOT
FOR FORD 8 H.P. CARS

Chromium Plated Finish. Eagle Mascot (1059F).
AM38A/905 ... ... each **12/6**

JAGUAR MASCOT
(MM521)

The very latest design. Ideal for the S.S. Jaguar Cars but suitable for all cars. A most faithful reproduction in heavy chromium-plated finish. 7½" length.
AM41B/3106 ... ... each **42/-**

"SPRITE" MASCOT

Height, 5". Length, 5½". All Chromium Finish.
AM36A/1809 ... ... each **25/-**

FLYING FISH MASCOT
(MM488)

Chromium finish. 5½" long, 4¼" width.
AM39B/905 ... ... each **12/6**

"SOCCER" MASCOT
(MM511)

5½" height. 3" width. Chromium-plated finish.
AM42B/1809 ... ... each **25/-**

G. T. RICHES & COMPANY, LIMITED

389. From the 1937 Riches catalogue, some of the stylised mascots available. Below centre, the leaping Jaguar, at this time S.S. cars were using the name Jaguar (post-war S.S. was dropped entirely, probably due to the connotations implied by the letters S.S.). Also of period interest is the golfer in plus fours, and the soccer player with knee-length shorts.

391. Not a Riley ski-lady, but an accessory skier mascot, chromium plated. Circa 1935.
£50 — £75

390. An above average example of a Riley ski-lady, chrome plated, bakelite radiator cap. 1930s.
£70 — £100

392. Lady golfer playing iron shot, nickel plated. Circa 1930.
£40 — £60

393. A golf caddy mascot by Frenay, chromium plated, 3½ins.:9cm high. Circa 1930.
£40 — £60

394. A Desmo golf ball in flight from tee and turf, chromium plated, on radiator cap mounting. 5ins.:12.5cm long, circa 1940. See golf ball on tee mascot also by Desmo, no. 422, p. 126.
£15 — £25

395. Small but impressive, a signed mascot by Palliot in the form of a cowboy who has leapt from his horse on to the back of a steer. Mounted on wooden plinth, the whole 6½ins.:16.5cm high.
£80 — £120

396. Equestrian mascots enjoyed a continuing period of popularity; here another version on a popular theme, plated horse, overpainted jockey. 1930s.

£30 — £50

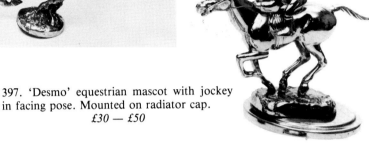

397. 'Desmo' equestrian mascot with jockey in facing pose. Mounted on radiator cap.

£30 — £50

398. Two post-war Desmo products, a 'Jockey's Success' equestrian mascot, 5½ins.:14cm high, and a 'Winning Greyhound', 6ins.:15cm long, both chromium plated and mounted on radiator caps.

£20 — £35 jockey
£20 — £35 greyhound

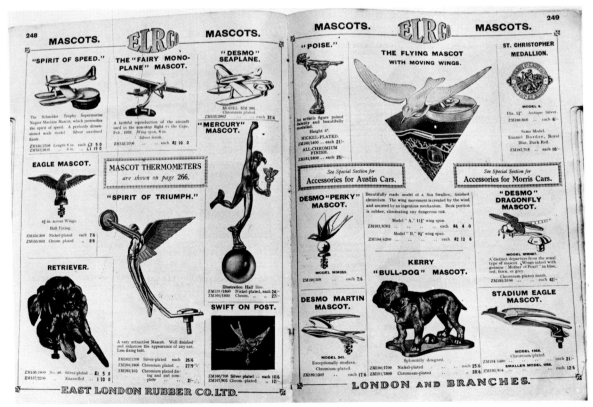

399. A selection of mid-'thirties mascots from the East London Rubber Company catalogue, with 'Spirit of Triumph', 'Desmo' dragonfly and others illustrated in this section.

400. A large and impressive chromium plated eagle mascot with wingspan of 9¾ins.:25cm, mounted on radiator cap, good quality. 1930s. (This type was popularly used on late Alvis cars.)

£50 — £75

401. Another eagle with outspread wings, note similarity to 400 (tail etc.). Attractive, but not such fine quality, plated. Circa 1930.

£30 — £60

402. Modelled on 'Puss in Boots' this amusing nickel plated novelty mascot of a seated kitten pulling on sea boots, has circular base stamped 'Hansie Siercke'. 5¼ins.:13.5cm high. 1920s.
£75 — £100

403. The coiled serpent by Desmo realistically poised about to strike, chromium plated. 1930s.
£30 — £40

404. Another serpent by another maker, in similar pose but not as realistic. 1930s.
£25 — £35

Colour Plate 6. Announcing the A.A.'s approval of a garage, a double-sided enamelled sign, shown here with original wall mounting bracket. 'Thirties.
£20 — £30

Colour Plate 8. Reassuring for R.A.C. members, a double-sided enamelled garage repairer's sign with its original mounting bracket. 'Twenties and 'thirties. See also no. 463, p.136.

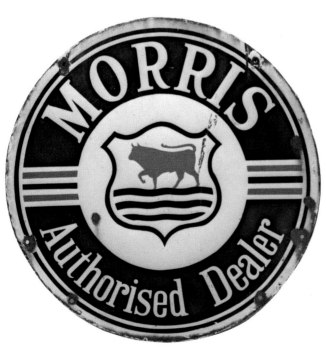

Colour Plate 7. A good pre-war Morris Authorised Dealer's enamelled sign, undamaged examples are scarce See also no. 448 on p. 133.

405. An impressive dragonfly mascot, plated brass and stamped 'MIERTIN' on the base. 1930s.
£60 — £90

406. The 'Bulldog', a popular British mascot, this time wearing goggles, chromium plated. Circa 1935.
£35 — £50

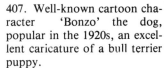

407. Well-known cartoon character 'Bonzo' the dog, popular in the 1920s, an excellent caricature of a bull terrier puppy.
£45 — £75

409. Again of 1930s stylised form, an aggressive looking cockatoo, plated brass.
£35 — £50

408. A bronze running Irish Wolfhound mascot, active style, but with flattened surfaces. 6¼ins.:16cm long.
£20 — £30

410. A powerful study of a wild boar, nickel plated. 3¾ins.: 9.5cm long. 1920s.
£35 — £50

411. Visually attractive, a plated squirrel with nut. 1930s.
£30 — £40

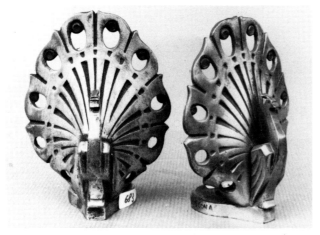

412. An interesting pair of stylised peacocks, stamped 'GEONA' on base. Circa 1930.
£40 — £60

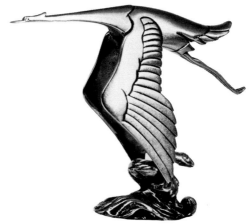

413. The stork in flight was an emblem adopted by Hispano Suiza, in honour of the French aviator George Guynemer whose squadron, Escadrille N.3, employed such a motif as their squadron badge during World War I. The stork illustrated is a high quality silver plated product. Some examples found are signed 'Bazin'; this example is unsigned. 7½ins.:19cm long and shown here mounted for display.
£75 — £100
£200 — £300 signed examples of certain provenance

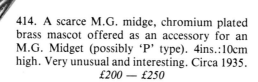

414. A scarce M.G. midge, chromium plated brass mascot offered as an accessory for an M.G. Midget (possibly 'P' type). 4ins.:10cm high. Very unusual and interesting. Circa 1935.
£200 — £250

415. Possibly intended as a mascot for Humber Snipe or Pullman cars, this stylised bird is mounted on pressed steel base with pennant mast.
£25 — £35

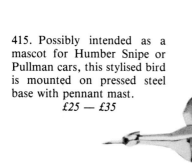

416. A leaping Jaguar S.S. car mascot by Desmo, see original catalogue illustration no. 389, p. 118. 8½ins.:20.5cm long. Circa 1937.
£30 — £50

418. A rather dramatic art deco mascot of a falcon about to take flight, brass plate. 4ins.:10cm high. 1930s.

£30 — £40

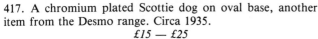

417. A chromium plated Scottie dog on oval base, another item from the Desmo range. Circa 1935.

£15 — £25

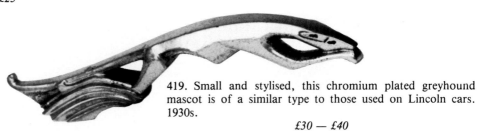

419. Small and stylised, this chromium plated greyhound mascot is of a similar type to those used on Lincoln cars. 1930s.

£30 — £40

420. Highly stylised, a Voisin mascot. An interesting construction, made from twelve pieces of polished aluminium sheet riveted together. This unusual arrangement reflects the firm's aeronautical involvement during World War I. Known as the 'Cocette'. 9ins.:23cm high. 1920s.

£80 — £120

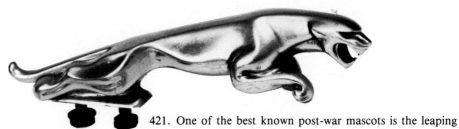

421. One of the best known post-war mascots is the leaping Jaguar, introduced by Jaguar cars in the mid-1950s, which first appeared on the 2.4 litre mark I. Chromium finish.

£10 — £15

DESMO MASCOTS

DESMO "DRAGONFLY"
(MM467)

Wings inlaid in genuine "Mother of Pearl".
Blue, red, fawn or grey. Chromium finish.
AM43A/3106   6¼" long   ...   ... each **42/-**

DESMO "SWIFT" MASCOT
(MM385)

Futurist design. Chromium finish. 5¼" high.
AM46A/905   ...   . each **12/6**

"FOX TERRIER" (MM469)

Chromium finish. 3" long.
AM49A/2206   ...   . each **30/-**

"DAWN" (MM475)

Chromium finish. 7¾" high.
AM44A/2802   ...   ...   each **37/6**
(MM476) 6½" high.
AM44B/1809 ...   .   each **25/-**

"GOLFBALL" MASCOT
(MM479)

Chromium finish. Coloured Tee. 2¼" high.
AM47A/1509   ...   . each **21/-**

"MARTIN" MASCOT
(MM341)

Futurist design. Chromium finish. 5½" long.
AM50A/1301   ...   ...   each **17/6**
As above. 4" long. MM341S.
AM50B/702   ...   . each **9/6**

"SEAPLANE" MASCOT
(MM386)

Chromium plated finish. 5½" long.
AM45A/2802   ...   . each **37/6**
MM387. As above, but 4½".
AM45B/1809   ...   . each **25/-**

DESMO "PERKY" MASCOT
(MM350)

Chromium finish. 2⅞" long.
AM48A/508   ...   . each **7/6**

"BULLDOG" MASCOT
(MM483)

Chromium finish. 4" long.
AM51A/2206   ...   . each **30/-**

19-21, STORE STREET, LONDON, W.C.1

422. Another page from the Riches catalogue, showing the Schneider Trophy Supermarine seaplane popular at the time as it held the world speed record at 406.99 m.p.h., and the Desmo 'Dragonfly', with wings of inlaid mother-of-pearl; undamaged, obviously very scarce.

423. An amusing safety pin mascot mounted on radiator cap and marked 'Safety first'. 5½ins.:14cm wide. Circa 1930.

£40 — £60

424. Unmistakably Bentley, a 'Flying B' mascot with outstretched wings to either side of letter. 8ins.:20cm wide, late 'twenties. Optional on the larger cars from Bentley's range (6½ and 8 litre models), and therefore a scarce and desirable item. Nickel plated.

£120 — £180

425. A forward sloping winged 'B' Bentley mascot from the mid-1930s, chromium plated, together with radiator cap; rearward sloping winged 'B' mascots exist, but are much scarcer as they had a short pre-war production life.

£25 — £40

426. Intended for use on the Bentley Mk. V (in production in 1939) a rare 'winged B' mascot of flowing form, chromium plated. The interruption of war resulted in only a handful of these cars being produced.

£150 — £200

427. Not quite a mascot, this radiator cap with cast wings provides additional leverage for tightening. 1930s.

£12 — £18

428. The famous French artist René Lalique produced a superb range of radiator cap mascots in glass, advertised as being 'almost unbreakable', and available with circular chrome bases capable of accommodating an electric bulb for night display. Such illuminated mascots with their opaque and polished glass give outstanding effects at night. Popular model produced in late 1920s could be obtained from £3. 3s. 0d. (£3.15) for unlighted models, to £4. 4s. 0d. (£4.20) for lighted models. The falcon mascot shown is of lighted base type, with the retailer's name and address to base, Breves Galleries, Knightsbridge, S.W.3. Circa 1928.

£400 — £600

429. Another Lalique falcon, this time without lit base. Circa 1928.
£300 — £450

430. One of Lalique's most famous opalescent glass mascots, 'Victoire' lighted type. 9½ins.:24cm long. Early 1920s.

£800 — £1,200

431. A Lalique grouse mascot of stylised design, again capable of illumination. Late 1920s.
£300 — £400

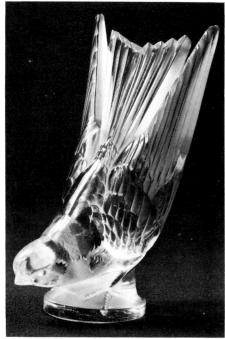

432. 'Epsom', a study of a horse's head in moulded glass by Lalique, circular plated base with side socket for electric illumination, stamped Breves Galleries. Radiator cap to base. 7ins:18cm high. Circa 1932. Note Lalique also produced another similar horse's head entitled 'Longchamps'.
£500 — £700

433. Another popular Lalique glass mascot 'Hirondelle', 4¼ins.:11cm high, signed R. Lalique, late 1920s; was also produced as a paperweight.

£150 — £250

434. Lalique's 'Cinq Chevaux' (five rearing horses) here shown with base for light; moulded signature clearly shown near base. Circa 1930.
£800 — £1,200

435. A dynamic Lalique glass car mascot entitled 'Tête de Bélier', the ram modelled with head lowered, the truncated curved neck terminating in a plain circular base, bearing the name 'R. Lalique France'. 3¾ins.:9.5cm high. Late 1920s. See also Colour Plate 4, p. 104.
£350 — £500

436. The Lalique ram's head mascot mounted on its nickel plated base clearly showing unusual underside bayonet socket for electrical fitting, usually found to side of mounting plinth.
£400 — £550

437. Clearly showing the artist's signature, this fine figure of a kneeling archer was entitled 'Tireur d'Arc'. 4ins.:10cm high, late 1920s.
£300 — £500

438. A Red Ashay illuminated glass mascot in the form of female head with flowing hair, note similarity to Lalique's 'Victoire' (no. 430), mounted on its lighting base with radiator cap fitting. Circa 1930.
£200 — £300

439. An attractive opaque glass mascot 'Butterfly Girl' by Red Ashay, shown here with radiator cap mounting. The base contains four colour filters, red, orange, blue, green, operated by selector to base (see above). English, late 1920s.
£300 — £400

440. Another Red Ashay glass mascot, their version of Lalique's 'Vitesse', nude female figure kneeling with hands holding flowing hair, base contains colour filters as previous item. 8¾ins.:22.5cm high. Circa 1930.
£300 — £400

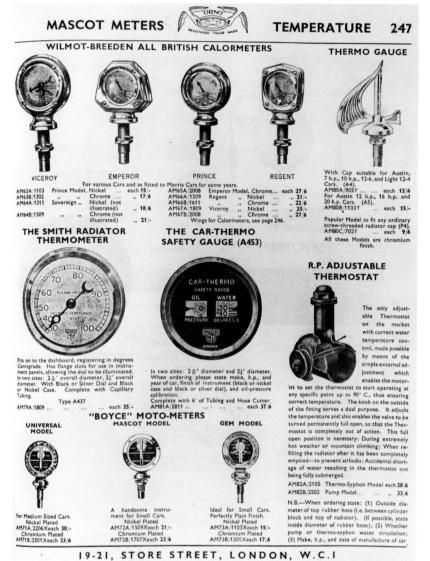

MASCOT METERS · ORNO REGISTERED TRADE MARK · TEMPERATURE 247

WILMOT-BREEDEN ALL BRITISH CALORMETERS · THERMO GAUGE

VICEROY · EMPEROR · PRINCE · REGENT

For various Cars and as fitted to Morris Cars for some years.

AM63A/1103 Prince Model, Nickel ... each 15/-
AM63B/1302 " Chrome ... " 17/6
AM64A/1311 Sovereign " Nickel (not illustrated) ... " 18/6
AM64B/1509 " Chrome (not illustrated) ... " 21/-

AM65A/2008 Emperor Model, Chrome... each 27/6
AM66A/1509 " Regent " Nickel ... " 21/-
AM66B/1611 " " Chrome ... " 22/6
AM67A/1809 " Viceroy " Nickel ... " 25/-
AM67B/2008 " " Chrome ... " 27/6
Wings for Calormeters, see page 246.

With Cap suitable for Austin, 7 h.p., 10 h.p., 12-6, and Light 12-4 Cars. (A4).
AM80A/90SY ... ... each 12/6
For Austin 12 h.p., 16 h.p. and 20 h.p. Cars. (A5).
AM80B/1103Y ... each 15/-

Popular Model to fit any ordinary screw-threaded radiator cap (P4).
AM80C/702Y ... each 9/6
All these Models are chromium finish.

THE SMITH RADIATOR THERMOMETER

Fits on to the dashboard, registering in degrees Centigrade. Has flange slots for use in instrument panels, allowing the dial to be illuminated. In two sizes: 2⅛" overall diameter, 2¼" overall diameter. With Black or Silver Dial and Black or Nickel Case. Complete with Capillary Tubing.
Type A437
AM79A/1809 ... ... each 25/-

THE CAR-THERMO SAFETY GAUGE (A453)

CAR-THERMO SAFETY GAUGE · OIL PRESSURE · WATER DEGREES C · LONDON

In two sizes: 2⅛" diameter and 2¼" diameter. When ordering please state make, h.p., and year of car, finish of instrument (black or nickel case and black or silver dial), and oil-pressure calibration.
Complete with 6' of Tubing and Hose Cutter.
AM81A/2811 ... ... each 37/6

R.P. ADJUSTABLE THERMOSTAT

The only adjustable Thermostat on the market with correct water temperature control, made possible by means of the simple external adjustment which enables the motorist to set the thermostat at any specific point up to 90° C., thus ensuring correct temperature. The knob on the outside of the fitting serves a dual purpose. It adjusts the temperature and also enables the valve to be turned permanently full open, so that the Thermostat is completely out of action. This full open position is necessary: During extremely hot weather or mountain climbing; When refilling the radiator after it has been completely emptied—to prevent airlocks; Accidental shortage of water resulting in the thermostat not being fully submerged.
AM82A/2105 Thermo-Syphon Model each 28/6
AM82B/2502 Pump Model... " 33/6

N.B.—When ordering state: (1) Outside diameter of top rubber hose (i.e. between cylinder block and top of radiator). (If possible, state inside diameter of rubber hose); (2) Whether pump or thermo-syphon water circulation; (3) Make, h.p., and date of manufacture of car

"BOYCE" MOTO-METERS

UNIVERSAL MODEL · MASCOT MODEL · GEM MODEL

For Medium Sized Cars. Nickel Plated
AM71A/2206Xeach 30/-
Chromium Plated
AM71B/2501Xeach 33/6

A handsome instrument for Small Cars. Nickel Plated
AM72A/1509Xeach 21/-
Chromium Plated
AM72B/1707Xeach 23/6

Ideal for Small Cars. Perfectly Plain Finish. Nickel Plated
AM73A/1103Xeach 15/-
Chromium Plated
AM73B/1301Xeach 17/6

19-21, STORE STREET, LONDON, W.C.I

441. A page from a 1937 Riches catalogue showing range of Wilmot-Breeden calormeters including the 'Viceroy' and the 'Regent' illustrated in the top row. Nickel and chrome finishes available.

442. Taking the place of the mascot, a Wilmot-Breeden 'Viceroy' calormeter giving driver instant radiator temperature information, in the days before pressurised cooling systems were introduced. Wings could be purchased separately and in illustration help to give 'mascot' effect.
£25 — £40

443. The 'Regent' calormeter as shown in catalogue in no. 441 but with mascot wings.
£20 — £25

444. An early M.G. Wilmot-Breeden calormeter, plated, forward facing glass bearing M.G. octagonal trademark (just visible). 7ins.:18cm high, late 1920s.

£40 — £60

445. Clearly showing 'Freezing, Cold, Normal and Boiling' this Wilmot-Breeden calormeter was mounted through radiator cap with part thermometer submerged in head tank water. 1920s.

£15 — £25

446. Intended for use on Mercedes cars, this three pointed star mascot incorporated a calormeter. 1920s.

£50 — £80

447. Mascot wings for calormeters as shown above, also mascots. Chromium plated versions were more expensive than silver plated. Also shown St. Christophers (see no. 322) and mascot brackets.

Enamel and Other Signs, Containers and Globes

A requirement for all automobiles is fuel and lubricating oil. The companies providing these products quickly realised the importance of advertising and produced colourful signs and posters. These are normally distinctive, with major companies adopting colours and emblems which have become their trademarks.

The collector will find a rich assortment of material in enamelled and lithographed finish as well as embossed. These metal items were obviously suitable for external display and, particularly with enamelled signs, some chipping may be present.

As plastic was yet to be accepted, fuel storage drums and cans were commonplace and of practical reusable form. Petrol was available in cans, usually two gallon type, bearing an embossed company emblem or name and were returnable (a charge of 3s. (15p) was levied against return of can).

Apart from metal or paper, glass featured prominently in the form of illuminated globes to surmount petrol pumps; these have almost disappeared since the 'fifties with the introduction of streamlined pumps.

449. A similar dealer/repairer enamelled sign for the French company Mathis. 1920s. £30 — £50

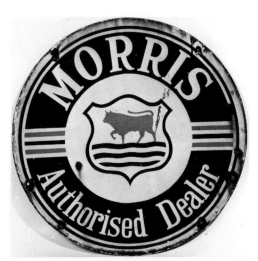

448. A Morris enamelled sign of the type displayed by Authorised Dealers, 1920s and 1930s. See also Colour Plate 7, p. 122.
£40 — £60

450. A double-sided right angled enamelled Pratt's Spirit sign finished in yellow, red and black. 1920s or 1930s. 21¼ins. × 21¼ins.:54cm × 54cm.
£20 — £30

451. Shown left, the enamel sign of a leading pre-war oil company, 'Pratts'. 1930s. Below, in red, white and blue, with cog edge, a Pratts circular double-sided enamelled advertising sign. 26ins.:66cm diameter, showing date code for 1930.

£35 — £50 each

452. The Union Jack is employed on this patriotic BP motor spirit sign, severe chipping to edges but still acceptable to the collector.

£15 — £25 condition poor

453. A double-sided Castrol enamel advertising sign, pre-war.

£15 — £20

454. A large size enamelled pre-war Castrol motor oil sign finished in green, white and red. Edges show signs of chipping, otherwise reasonable condition.

£15 — £20

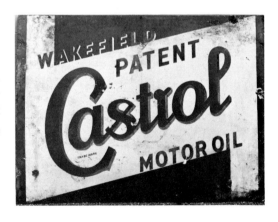

455. Two impressive and visually deceptive advertising signs. Far left, flat tinplate oil drum was used as an advertising sign with the slogan 'Save Trouble, Buy Castrol By the Drum'. The price of Castrol 'R' (famed for its distinctive smell) was 45s. 10d. (£2.29) for 5 gallons. Finished in traditional Castrol colours, mid-1930s. See also Colour Plate 10, p. 139. Left, a realistic 'shaped' double-sided enamelled Shell advertising sign in the form of an oil can. 15¾ins.:40cm wide. Late 1920s. See also back dust jacket.

£35 — £50 Castrol}
£40 — £60 Shell} *seldom encountered*

456. A large 'Shell' enamel sign for general advertising purposes.

£12 — £15 condition poor

457. An oval shaped Esso ethyl enamel sign. Pre-war.
£20 — £30

458. 'Alcohol for Engine Power' was Cleveland's slogan on this pre-war petrol sign.

£20 — £30

459. Using the words 'Dunlop stock' to imply a range of Dunlop products available, e.g. tyres, tubes, pumps, gauges, hoses, etc. Enamelled in black, red and yellow. 1930s.
£20 — £30

460. The more recognisable post-war BP sign, printed on tin, less durable than enamel.

£15 — £25

461. Another printed sign, this time showing the fading and scratching encountered where paint is used externally. Exide Batteries sign, 1940s.

£15 — £20

Above right: 462. The Road Transport & General Insurance Company Limited, advertising insurance for the motorist, a pre-war sign enamelled in chocolate brown, green and cream.

£25 — £40

Right: 463. A bracket mounted R.A.C. approved repairer garage sign. 1930s. See also Colour Plate 8, p. 122.

£20 — £30

464. Probably from pre-World War I, when local authorities enforced varying speed limits through towns and villages, a 10 m.p.h. speed limit sign. Cast iron.

£30 — £50

465. Before the days when local authorities produced adequate warning signs, motoring organisations contributed. Here a pre-World War II Automobile Association and Motor Union motorist warning notice, showing distressed enamel. See also no. 777, p. 238.

£15 — £20

466. An Ocean Motor Policies 'Light Up Today' tin sign, of clock form with movable hands, 14¼ins.:36cm diameter. 1920s.

£25 — £40

467. For use with petrol pumps, this Shellmex price ticket holder was produced in 'Shell' shape. The amount of Government tax is clearly indicated. The butterfly nut and hinged top for replacement price tickets would be fitting to today's erratic pricing.

£25 — £40

468. A Bowser hand operated petrol pump, dial indicating 15 gallon maximum delivery capacity, by which time the operator's arm would be very tired. Provision for globe (missing) to hood. Circa 1920.

£80 — £120

469. Not free standing but wall mounted, this petrol pump P17240 Mark IVc produced single gallon delivery from twin glazed reservoirs, brass digital gallon recorder, reciprocating pump handle, shown here with pipe, nozzle and parts. Circa 1920.

£60 — £100

470. Of the type still discovered on farms, transport yards, etc., a Bowser hand operated petrol pump, cast iron with brass cylinder. 1920s.

£40 — £60

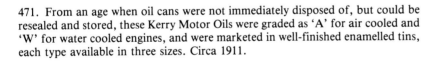

471. From an age when oil cans were not immediately disposed of, but could be resealed and stored, these Kerry Motor Oils were graded as 'A' for air cooled and 'W' for water cooled engines, and were marketed in well-finished enamelled tins, each type available in three sizes. Circa 1911.

472. Dating of cans can be made easy by inspection of base. Major can manufacturers stamped their name, month and last two digits of year to bottom of can. Here shown, above right, a good example of a Shell 2 gallon petrol can finished in black with gilt 'Shell' motif, 1931. Right, an attractive Pratts 2 gallon petrol can dated for 1926, finished in black with gilt lettering. The top of can also bears an embossed 3s. (15p) deposit.

£18 — £25 Shell }
£18 — £25 Pratts } *both in original condition, not restored*

Colour Plate 9. Advertising Dunlop tyres, a single-sided enamel wall sign in traditional Dunlop colours. Pre-war.
£30 — £50

Colour Plate 10. Castrol's deceptive drum advertising sign with its clever slogan. See also no. 455 on p. 134.

Colour Plate 11. An enamelled shield-shaped advertising sign for Humber Cars. 'Twenties.

£35 — £50

473. A selection of 2 gallon brass petrol caps, note variety of companies including Pratts, Shell, Esso, Anglo American, etc. 1920s.

£1 — £3

474. Known as the Mobiloil 'Cone' using embossed Gargoyle motif, this 2½ gallon container is for 'BB' grade (equivalent to grade 40 oil). 1930s.

£2 — £4

475. Heavy oils for use in axles and some gearboxes were produced by the major companies. Shown here a Pratts tractor oil 5 gallon can. Enamelled tins are more popular than those bearing paper labels. 1930s.

£2 — £4

476. Bearing their 'Gargoyle' trademark, a late 1930s 'Mobiloil' 5 gallon oil drum 'BB' (this oil was recommended for summer use, and for sports cars in winter). Price with oil in 1937 £1. 13s. 9d. (£1.69).

£2 — £4

477. A Shell 1 gallon oil can finished in black with red and yellow, the white disc at side would have been overstamped with grade of oil. Original cap. Circa 1930.

£10 — £15

478. Much scarcer than the usual 5 gallon can, a Redline-Glico 1 gallon oil can finished in black with red and yellow. 'Thirties.

£6 — £10

479. A 1 gallon Aeroshell oil can, a product recommended for Aero engines and high precision motor car and motor cycle engines, and officially approved by Rolls-Royce. Attractively enamelled in red, yellow and black. Circa 1930.

£10 — £15

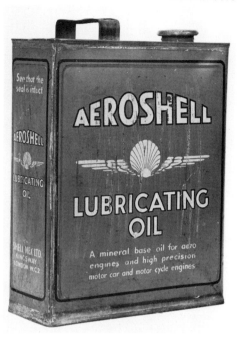

480. An embossed 5 gallon oil drum bearing 'Castrol' trademark, grade of oil (XL) painted on can. Pre-war.

£3 — £6

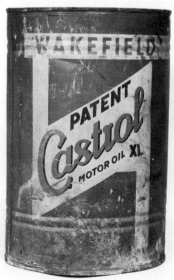

481. A later Castrol 5 gallon oil drum with printed trademark. Post-war.

£3 — £6

482. Not all oil came in cans, Esso favoured bottles; here a pre-war quart container of distinctive design.

£1 — £2 each

Colour Plate 12. Also producers of automobile and aircraft tyres, Palmer was a leading company of tyre producers, pre-war. This 1913 double-sided board advertising sign emphasises quality. Note each side of the board has a different illustration, right and below.

£20 — £30

Left: Colour Plate 13. A Ballonettes tyres advertising sign. 'Thirties.

£30 — £40

Above: Colour Plate 14. A GWK Maidenhead advertising sign. 'Thirties.

£30 — £40

29, & 31. Gt. Eastern St. London.

LUBRICANTS—continued.
OILS AND GREASE.

MOEBIUS.

		1-Qt. Tins. each.	½-Gal. Tins. each.	1-Gal. Tins. each.
XL917	Mark H. Air cooled	2/2	3/8	6/0
XL918	„ M. Water „	2/2	3/8	6/0
XL919	„ LL. „	2/2	3/8	6/0
XL920	Gear Oil ...	—	—	6/0

GREASE.
"KERRY."

XL921	2-lb. tins ...	...	each	1/8
XL922	4 „ „	...	„	3/0
XL923	7 „ „	...	„	4/6

"G.B." Motor Oil.

No. 1.—A medium-bodied oil, suitable for water-cooled engines of the lower speeds.

XL924	Quart tins ...	...	per doz.	20/0
XL925	½-gallon tins	...	„	36/0
XL926	1 gallon „	...	„	60/0
XL927	5 or 10 gallon drums, per gall.			3/4
XL928	Barrels ...	...	„	3/2

No. 2.—A full-bodied oil of exceptional viscosity, suitable for high-speed engines.

XL929	Quart tins ...	...	per doz.	22/0
XL930	½-gallon tins	...	„	40/0
XL931	1 gallon „	...	„	68/0
XL932	5 or 10 gallon drums, per gall			4/0
XL933	Barrels ...	...	„	3/10

"G.B."

			Per doz.
XL934	Motor Grease, 1-lb. tins...		10/0
XL935	„ „ 2-lb. „ ...		20/0
XL936	„ „ 7-lb. „ ...		56/0
XL937	„ „ ... per cwt.		60/0

Vacuum Grease.

XL938 Vacuum Mobilubricant.

14-lbs.	7-lbs.	4-lbs.	2-lb.	1-lb.
117/0	64/0	36/0	22/6	12/0 per doz.

XL939 Vacuum Graphite Grease.

14 lbs.	7-lbs.	4-lbs.	2-lbs.	1-lb.
144/0	90/0	54/0	30/0	18/0 per doz.

STAUFFERS' GREASE.

XL940	1-lb. tins ...	...	each	1/6
XL941	2 „ „ ...	...	„	2/6
XL942	4 „ „ ...	...	„	4/8
XL943	7 „ „ ...	...	„	7/6
XL944	14 „ „ ...	...	„	15/0
XL945	28 „ kegs ...	...	„	28/0
XL946	56 „ „ ...	...	„	49/0

Kegs 6/- extra—Returnable.

197

483. Oil and grease tins pre-World War I. Where printing includes representation of an automobile, prices will be higher than for plainer types. Additional competition, especially for small sizes, will come from the general collector of tins.

484. A good pre-war Texaco quart measure with wide pouring lip.

£4 — £7

485. Finished in red, yellow and black, this attractive Shell quart oil measure bears Weights and Measures stamp, a crowned 'GR 30', for 1930.
£4 — £7

486. A post-war Castrol pint oil measure, note 'GR' Weights and Measures seal near lip confirming standard capacity and dated '51' for 1951.

£3 — £5

487. A selection of anti-freeze and oil measures, circa 1930-50.
£2 — £4

488. A selection of 1930s oil containers of different types. Left to right: Castrol screw-top one quart capacity, Luvax shock absorber fluid with combined cap and spout and a Smith's Jackall hydraulic fluid for built-in jacks.

£2 — £3   £3 — £5   £1 — £2

489. Displaying the famous 'Gargoyle' trademark, a tin of Mobil Mobilgrease No. 5 for metal universal joints. Frequently these cans are found to be in excellent condition when carefully cleaned as their contents prevent rust. 1930s.

£1 — £2

490. Though not a motor product, this Junior Shell lighter fuel can follows the style of large fuel cans. Enamelled finish red, yellow and black. 4¾ins.:12cm high. 1930s.

£3 — £5

480 'BROWN BROTHERS, Limited

Oilers.

The "Duco" Seamless Steel Oil Cans.

The body is formed out of one steel sheet, impossible to leak, solid steel valves, brass seats, steel springs fitted without solder, will not get out of order.

Heavy gauge pattern.

No. O1/1. Capacity, ½ pint, 6 in. spouts ... ... *each 1/6
,, O1/2. ,, ¼ ,, 7 in. ,, ... 1/8
,, O1/3. ,, ¾ ,, 8 in. ,, ... 1/10
,, O1/4. ,, 1 ,, 9 in. ,, ... 2/3

Oil Cans.

A well made tin plate oil can at a low price. Fitted with tinned iron slide feed holes.
Bottoms are seamed on by machine and then soldered.

No. O1/6. Size ½ pint ... ... each 1/1
,, O1/7. ,, ¾ 1/2
,, O1/8. ,, ¾ 1/3

The "Duco" Seamless Squirt Oil Can.

Fitted with force pump for ejecting the oil in any direction.

No. O1/12. ½ pint ... ... each 3/3
,, O1/13. ¾ ,, ... ,, 3/9

The "Duco" Detachable Spout Seamless Steel Oil Can.
These cans are special value.
No. O1/ 0. Capacity, ½ pint, 7 in. spouts (tin) ... each 2/2

"Kaye's" Serrated Steel Seamless Oil Cans.
No. O1/14. Capacity, ½ pint. No. 16 ... each 2/-
,, O1/15. ,, ¾ ,, ,, 17 ... ,, 2/3
,, O1/16. ,, ¾ ,, ,, 18 ... ,, 2/6

"Kaye's" Oblong Steel Oil Can.
With seamed bottom.
No. O1/17. Capacity, ½ pint No. 14a. ... each 1/6
,, O1/18. ,, ¾ ,, ,, 13a. ... ,, 1/9
,, O1/19. ,, ¾ ,, ,, 12a. ... ,, 2/3

The "Duco" Ordinary Oil Can, Taper Loco Pattern Fixed Spout, Double Valves.

No. O1/21. "Duco Midget." Tinned steel,
10 in. overall ... ... each 2/6
,, O1/22. Steel, length 18 in. overall ... ,, 2/9
,, O1/23. ,, ,, 24 in. ,, ... ,, 3/6
NOTE.—The "Midget" is an extremely handy size for the tool box, and sells in large quantities.

"Duco" Seamless Bench Oil Can.
Heavy gauge well tinned.
Shallow type.
5 in. spout, ¼ pint.
No. O1/24. ... each -/9
6 in. spout, ½ pint.
No. O1/25. ... each 1/-

"Duco" Engineer's Midget Size Oil Can.
British manufacture. Well and strongly made.
A neat and useful size for the tool box.
No. O1/20. Capacity, ¼ pint ... ... each 1/1

The "Duco" Oil Filler.
A pattern that is greatly used in workshops, etc., made of heavy gauge material.
Strongly finished.

each
No. O1/26. Capacity, 1 pint 1/4
,, O1/27. ,, 2 ,, 2/-

"Record" Motor Oiler.
Strong and well made handy design, will stand upright in tool box.
Length, 10 in.
No. O1/28. Brass ... ... each 2/-
,, O1/29. Plated ... ... ,, 2/3

Please quote List Numbers and give full particulars when Ordering.

London Manchester Paris

491. Just as early cycles carried a small oiler in their tool kit, so too did many early motorists. The 'Duco', top left, is typical of cans employed for minor maintenance, circa 1911. Note 'Kaye's' serrated steel seamless oil can (centre right), a miniature of this type was later offered as a Hornby Railway accessory in 1938 at a cost of 3s. 6d. (17½p). Note also 'Duco' oil filler (lower left).

492. A good brass Lucas No. 40 forced feed oil can. A spring clip could be supplied to carry oil can on bulkhead of car. The spring clip is just visible on finger ring to hold screw cap when in use. 1920s and 1930s.
£12 — £15

493. Shown here held in its can carrier by retaining spring, a 'Braime' oiler circa 1930. The shape had changed little from the previous twenty years.
£8 — £12

494. Another oiler by the same maker, this time a brass framed carrier, with detachable spout. Carriers considerably enhance value.
£8 — £12

495. A selection of oil cans, drip trays and other accessories from a 1934 E.L.R. Co. catalogue, showing gear oil bucket, and 'Mac-Stan' oiler with flexible extension.

496. An Enots No. 10A high pressure brass oil can, with press pump, refillable at end. Circa 1930. See no. 495 for illustration of similar model.

£4 — £6

497. A Jeavons oil gun in brass of syringe-like design, a well made period accessory. 1920s.

£7 — £10

498. A good quality functional nickel plated fuel funnel. 1920s and 1930s.

£2 — £4

A further specialised collecting area may be found in the field of petrol pump globes produced in glass, mounted on top of pumps and illuminated at night by an internal bulb. Shown here are some from the 1930s, war-time and post-war periods.

499. A Pratts Benzol Mixture globe, white with plain black lettering. Pre-war.

£25 — £35

500. Using a globe of similar shape, this time BP Commercial (lower grade petrol). Pre-war.

£20 — £30

501. 'Not for Resale', a globe used on farm or private company pumps. Pre-war.

£20 — £30

502. This pre-war 'Shell' globe in traditional shell shape carries 'Pool' sticker. During World War II individual companies all contributed to the national stockpile of petroleum spirit and the word pool came into use. The product is remembered as a low octane (approx. 80 octane) fuel and had a reputation for valve burning.

£25 — £40

503. A pre-war Dominion globe, white with blue edging, also with war-time 'Pool' sticker.

£25 — £40

504. A post-war Shell Economy pump globe, this fuel was roughly equivalent to today's two-star petrol (approx. 93 octane).

£15 — £25

505. 'Shellmex'; another post-war globe equivalent to 3 or 4 star (approx. 97 octane).

£15 — £25

507. The equivalent to Super Shell was BP Super, green shield with white lettering. 1950s.

£15 — £25

506. 'Super Shell', 101 octane, an equivalent to 5 star grade.

£15 — £25

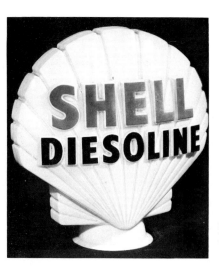

508. For the commercial vehicle, Shell Diesoline, post-war.

£15 — £25

Manufacturers' Publicity Material (including Catalogues)

Popular for some time has been the collecting of car manufacturers' catalogues; these vary considerably in quality and content and some very high standards of artwork and design are encountered. Catalogues from the 'twenties and 'thirties are particularly attractive.

In the 'thirties, particularly, the major oil companies produced give-away leaflets and booklets claiming the merits of their products; these either took the form of amusing visual ephemera or more serious booklets listing competition achievements.

Highly artistic posters covering all forms of motoring may be encountered, many by leading artists of the period, though due to large size and vulnerability, undamaged examples of these may be scarce.

509. The American company Nordyke & Marmon produced this high quality catalogue of coachwork available for the Marmon chassis. Obviously a catalogue aimed at the wealthy. The quality illustration, right, is taken from the catalogue and shows a body produced for Mrs. Richard Olney of Boston. 1920s.

£50 — £80

510. Again for the very rich, this Hispano-Suiza catalogue, with finely coloured drawings, is one of a limited edition of five hundred. A rare and desirable item. Above, inside cover details; below, two examples of bodies available on the 54 h.p. chassis. Circa 1932.

£300 — £400

511. Not exactly a catalogue, but a review of 'expert opinions' concerning the new 20 h.p. Rolls-Royce car, of particular interest to Rolls-Royce collectors and very scarce. Circa 1923.

£20 — £30

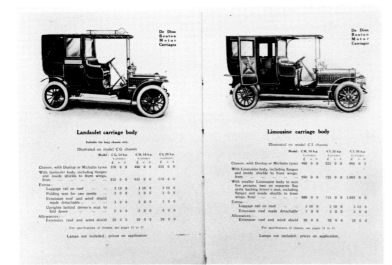

512. Two pages from a scarce De Dion Bouton catalogue, Publication No. 199, February 1910, 32 pages, 10 with illustrations. Note, 'lamps not included'.

£30 — £40

513. Two good quality Humber catalogues from the mid-1920s, showing typical period coachwork. Above, 1925; below, with monochrome cover, 1927. —
£15 — £25 each

514. 'Twenties catalogue for the Vauxhall 20-60 open tourer. Vauxhall were one of the first motor car manufacturers to introduce syncromesh gearboxes.
£15 — £25

515. Two Aston Martin catalogues of the mid-1930s. Above, a book-type double page catalogue for the Mark II Sports illustrating open and closed versions; and below a single sheet catalogue for the new 'Ulster' Model guaranteeing maximum speed of 100 m.p.h.
£15 — £25

516. Two mid-1930s catalogues. Above, Singer poster-type catalogue illustrating four versions of 9 h.p. cars, the cover claiming the firm to be the first to introduce fluid drive and independent front wheel suspension. Below, a Lagonda Rapier double fold catalogue giving details of sports saloon and sports tourer, cover 9ins.:23cm wide. See also Colour Plate 16, p. 159.

£10 — £15 Singer   £35 — £50 Lagonda

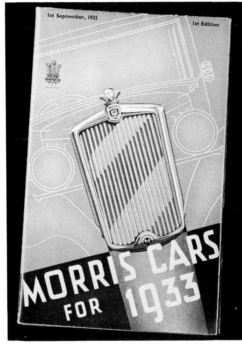

517. A Morris Cars catalogue for 1933, cover showing interesting Morris signal indicator (traffic light style) visible on nearside windscreen pillar. First edition, issued 1st September 1932.

£10 — £15

518. The front cover for an M.G. 'T' series Midget catalogue 1937, 9ins.:23cm wide. See also Colour Plate 15, p. 159.

£25 — £40

519. The inside cover and first page of no. 518, showing Sir Malcolm Campbell driving an M.G. in the J.C.C. International Trophy 1935.

520. Two varieties of catalogue for the Talbot 'Three Litre' car, both stamped with local dealers' details. 1938.
£10 — £15 each

521. A 1937 Austin Eighteen and Twenty Model catalogue with imitation basketweave cover, tied-in sheets, body styles illustrated.

£10 — £15

522. This stylish Chrysler catalogue with silver cover illustrates the '72' model. 1930s.
£22 — £28

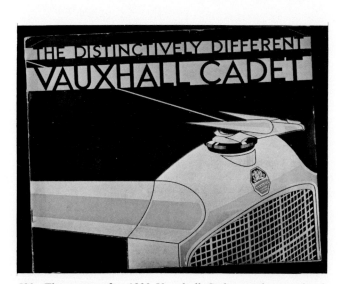

523. The cover of a 1933 Vauxhall Cadet catalogue, simple and uncluttered, emphasising the 'Distinctively Different' claim.

£10 — £15

524. Not just a catalogue for one model, but one giving the range of cars offered by Hillman for the 1939 season.
£10 — £15

525. Three further mid-1930s catalogues. Left, Humber 'Twelve' 1934 with colourful interior of poster-type showing three styles of bodywork. Centre, claiming to be 'The Car of Tomorrow — Today', the Airstream Singer Eleven, twelve page catalogue, note the resemblance of this car to the Chrysler Airflow. Right, a poster-type catalogue for Humber's new models, 16/60, Snipe 80 and Pullman, open poster size 30ins.:76cm wide. 1934.

£10 — £15 each

526. A 1935 Renault catalogue covering the range from 12.1 to 32 h.p. and depicting the very stylish Super Airline Saloon. Also shown, companion price list (cover for catalogue same as price list).

£10 — £15

527. In green, black and white, this Armstrong Siddeley catalogue for the 1935 range includes details of six models with prices from £265 to £1,360. Note pre-selector gear change lever to steering wheel.

£10 — £15

528. Although not entirely clear from the photograph, this promotional card had a lift-up section to reveal major components of the Standard 'Ensign' Six. Circa 1930.

£5 — £8

529. Standard Cars' catalogues for 1935. Above, book type catalogue; below, folded type catalogue, each covering the 1935 range. Prices ranged from £145 to £395. Note, these are smaller type catalogues, 5ins.:13cm wide.

£8 — £12

530. Differing cover designs for 1930s catalogues. Note, lower right, British Salmson winged radial engine with propellor motif on imitation crocodile grained cover; also Hillman catalogue, top right, with car climbing hill.
£6 — £9 each Trojan and Hillman
£10 — £15 each Humber
Vauxhall £6 — £9   British Salmson £12 — £18

531. Copies of this early Rolls-Royce catalogue have been reprinted and potential buyers should be careful to confirm authenticity. Originally issued with a postcard, ten vehicles illustrated within. 1905.
£50 — £80 original   £4 — £6 copy

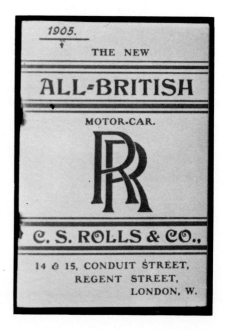

1905.

THE NEW

ALL=BRITISH

MOTOR-CAR.

RR

C. S. ROLLS & CO.,

14 & 15, CONDUIT STREET,
REGENT STREET,
LONDON, W.

532. More of a brochure than a catalogue, Belsize Motors produced this to illustrate their delivery vans, charming styles. Shown open. Circa 1912.
£8 — £12

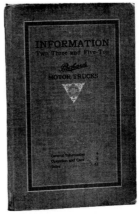

533. On the left, information (instruction) for the Two, Three and Five-ton Packard motor truck 1913. This contains general information for operation and care. The cover motif incorporates slogan 'Ask the man who owns one'. On the right, a Packard information manual issued for the Packard Eight in February 1925.
£15 — £25 each

534. A selection of A.C. (Auto-Carriers) printed material including catalogue, handbook and promotional postcard, and an A.C. advertising transfer with original instructions for affixing to glass. Circa 1916.
£25 — £40 catalogue only

535. A selection of very useful motor accessory catalogues: The Taylor Catalogue 'Everything Motorish...' 1914, Gamage's Motoring Department Catalogue 1915, and three small size Brown Bros. Catalogues, top 1913, middle 1916, (cover states 'Issued under war conditions'), below 1920.

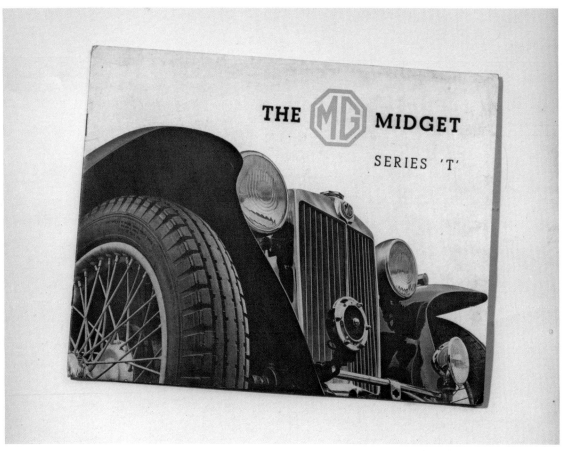

Colour Plate 15. A simple but effective catalogue cover for the MG 'T' series Midget, 1937.
See also no. 518 on p. 154.

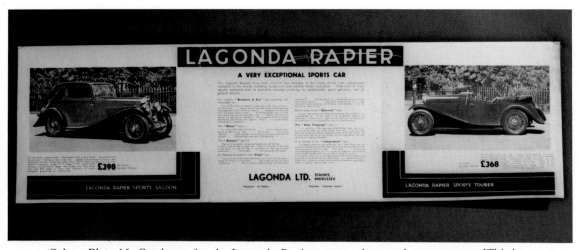

Colour Plate 16. Catalogue for the Lagonda Rapier sports saloon and sports tourer. 'Thirties.
See also no. 516, p. 154.

536. In addition to handbooks and workshop manuals, illustrated spare parts lists provide useful information; shown here a Morris Oxford and Cowley issued 1st January, 1930, and a Standard 1938 parts list.

£8 — £12 each

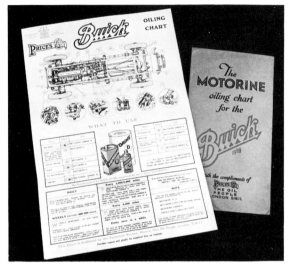

537. Given free by Price's to promote Motorine oil, an oiling chart for a 1929 Buick presented in its own envelope.

£5 — £8

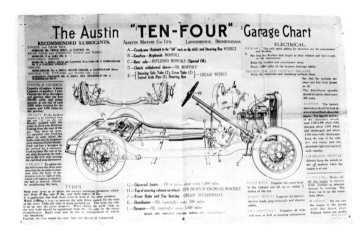

538. A mid-1930s Austin 'Ten-Four' Garage lubrication wall chart with diagram and instructions.

£5 — £8

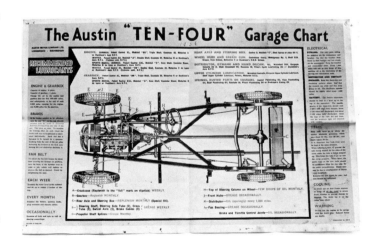

539. A similar lubrication wall chart for the same model, slight variations to above.

£5 — £8

Colour Plate 17. More of a poster than catalogue, this Vauxhall range for 1934 opens out to a large 38ins. × 26½ins.:97 × 67cm poster showing Light Six, Big Six and Limousine.
£15 — £25

Colour Plate 18. The reverse (front) of the above with welcoming lady, synchromesh details, and 'For healthier motoring, no draught ventilation' advertisement.

540. Castrol produced booklets with dramatic covers listing achievements in the world of speed using Castrol oil. Well illustrated, 1933, 50 pages; 1934, 56 pages.
£5 — £8 each

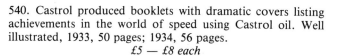

541. Entitled 'The Modern Motor Car' this Shell-Mex and BP publication effectively conveys the workings and construction of a motor car with lift-up sectional diagram, and numbered identification. Note illustration of chassis. Circa 1934.
£12 — £18

542. As a companion volume to 541, another publication entitled 'The Modern Commercial Vehicle' included similar diagrams and information.
£15 — £25

543. Continuing the theme of producing promotional achievement booklets, National Benzole issued this version for 1935 and claimed 'to be the ideal Motor Spirit — on the track, in the air, on the road'. Various achievements recorded with illustrations.

£4 — £6

544. A more practical advertising poster by Michelin advertising their 'Zigzag Stop' de luxe tyre, showing salesman's sample block of tyre section overlaid.
£4 — £6

 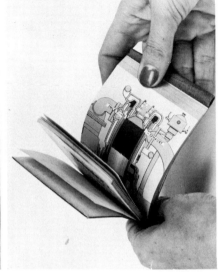

545. Two illustrations of a cinematograph booklet produced by Daimler C. depicting in diagrammatic form the workings of a sleeve valve engine. 64 pages showing each of the four cycles, cloth covered. Interesting. 1920s.
£10 — £15

546. Essolube's answer to Castrol's 'Achievements' was called, with some originality, 'Successolubes'. Well illustrated, 1936.

£4 — £6

547. Essolube produced this 'fly-up' promotional leaflet which, when opened, caused mechanic's arm to raise bottle. 11½ins.:29cm wide open. 1930s.
£1 — £2

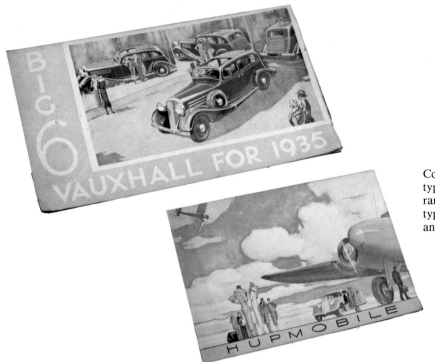

Colour Plate 19. Above, a Vauxhall poster-type catalogue, here shown folded, Big Six range 1935. Below, another 'thirties book-type catalogue for the Hupmobile series 421 and 427 models, 1934.

£15 — £25 Vauxhall
£12 — £18 Hupmobile

Colour Plate 20. Two Humber catalogues: above, issued in 1934, the full range illustrated in colour, well detailed, small size 36 page book-type with price list and colour schemes. Below, a small size 32 page book-type catalogue issued 1933, similar. 5¾ins.:14.5cm wide.

£10 — £15 each

Colour Plate 21. An interesting blend of colours is used with this Connolly artwork for the 1933 MG Magnette; note use of 'Safety fast' slogan. Shown with the inside of 1933 MG J2 Midget catalogue.
£30 — £50 each

Colour Plate 22. Inside of MG Magnette catalogue for 1933 and Connolly designed covers for MG Midget, and specification for J4 Midget and K3 Magnette Racing models.
£60 — £80
K3 Magnet Racing Model

548. Another clever Essolube promotion gimmick with concealed rotating colour disc to imitate pouring of oil into sump. Two illustrations to show full and near empty bottle. 1930s.
£3 — £5

549. Two educational booklets produced to promote oil products. Left, a Castrol 52 page sponsored guide; right, a Motorine 47 page guide. 1930s.
£1.50 — £2.50 each

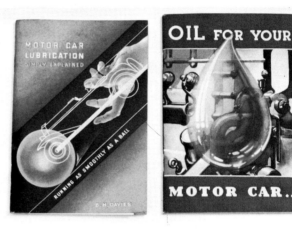

550. Perhaps proving the claim that advertising pays, yet another Castrol oil booklet mentioning that 39 out of 43 British makers advise Castrol (20 pages). 'Thirties.
£2 — £4

551. A selection of 1930s brochures, including Price's Patent Candle Company Ltd. 'Oil and engine wear', Castrol 'Save your car from the tow-rope', Essolube 'Motor Oil', Hillman Aero Minx 'A new thrill has come into life', and National Benzole 'It pays to buy British Benzole'.
£1.50 — £2.50 each

552. 'Perfection in a Nut-Shell', a claim for Daimler fluid flywheel transmission, colourful flip-up folder. 1930s.
£1.50 — £2.50

553. 'Priceless to the Motorist' was this *Pratts Pictorial,* a seasonal paper produced by the Petroleum Company as a give-away to customers. News and articles of motoring interest, also proclaiming the merits of Pratts High Test fuel, Essolube, etc.
£1 — £2

554. Another selection of 1930s promotional leaflets, including Desmo 'Safebeam' lamps, Pratts 'Daily Tellacram' (High Test petrol), Daimler 'Fluid Flywheel Transmission' and Serck Radiators Ltd. (Manufacturers' and Repairers' Services).
£1.50 — £2.50

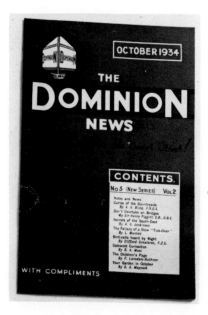

555. Dominion petrol produced this magazine for the owner driver, 24 pages, various articles. October 1934.
£1 — £2

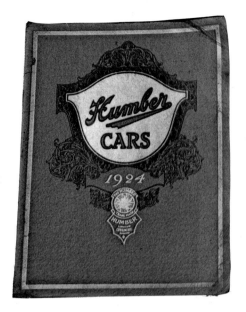

Colour Plate 23. Far left, a high quality Humber catalogue covering the 1924 range with embossed name to cover, 28 pages comprehensively illustrated. 8¼ins.:21cm wide. Also shown, an Olympia Show number of *Roadcraft,* October 1933, a magazine with articles and advertising issued by the Smith Group of Companies.
£5 — £8 *Roadcraft*   £25 — £40 *Humber*

Colour Plate 24. A 1934 Hillman catalogue showing Club Saloon and Sports Tourer.
£10 — £15

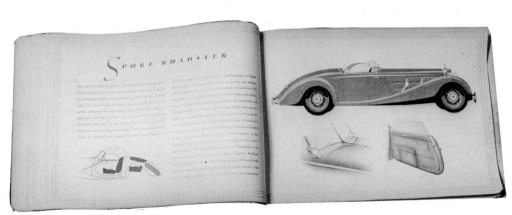

Colour Plate 25. A Mercedes catalogue illustrating Sports Roadster model. Circa 1937.
£100 — £150

556. A National Benzole promotional racing record booklet, a Hillman Minx explanation of the Minx all synchromesh gearbox, and a Sternol oil company 'First aid for the Car', mid-1930s.

£1.50 — £2.50 each

557. A puzzle folder inviting one to find 'Fort Dunlop' (note instructions on cover), and a realistic cut-out Gamage battery promotional booklet/catalogue, mid-1930s.

£2 — £3 each

558. A 'Triplex' safety glass price list for June 1934, and a Smith's Batteries catalogue, 1934.

£1 — £2 each

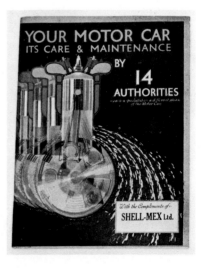

559. Shell-Mex recruited fourteen authorities on motor cars to contribute specialised articles on driving and maintenance in this complimentary booklet. Extremely interesting articles and useful information. 56 pages. Circa 1930.

£3 — £5

Colour Plate 26. A fine watercolour by Rene Vincent depicting Lincoln Saloon, 16¼ins. × 9½ins.:41.5cm
× 24cm. Original artwork for advertisement for *L'Illustration*, 1925.
£400 — £500

Colour Plate 27. An example of original artwork by Connolly for an 'M' type MG sports car,
15ins. × 8¼ins.:38cm × 21cm. Circa 1930. See also 562, p. 172.

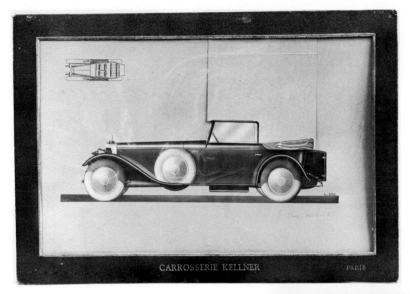

560. Left and below, an example of a fine quality early coachbuilder's coloured artwork for Mercedes, with lift-up section to convey hood in raised and lowered position. Signed Georges Kellner et Fils, French. Mid- to late 1920s.

£50 — £75

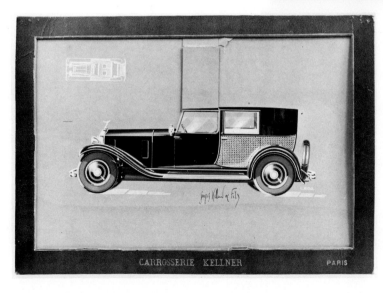

561. From the same studio, an example of coachwork for Rolls-Royce, with lift-up section to forward compartment, signed as above.

£50 — £75

562. High quality original artwork, possibly for use by manufacturers in catalogue, an MG 'M' type Midget of 1931 signed Connolly, depicted in Kentish countryside. 15ins. × 8¼ins.:38cm × 21cm. See also Colour Plate 27, p. 170.
£300 — £400

LA GRANDE MÉNAGERIE AUTOMOBILE DE LA RUE D'ANJOU

563. A French colour poster depicting gentleman in heavy motoring coat, with selection of cars including Oldsmobile and Hotchkiss. Circa 1908.
£5 — £10

564. A screen print by Claude Fligat depicting racing cars negotiating banked section of circuit. 15ins. × 17ins.:38cm × 43cm.
£60 — £100

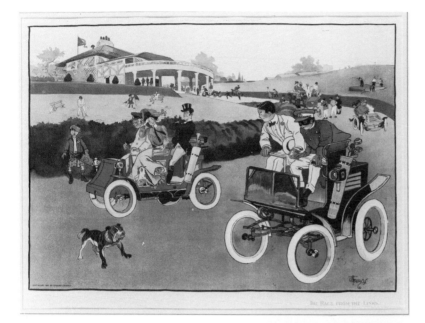

565. Entitled 'The Race from the Links', a fine coloured print by Stuart Travis, copyright 1901, depicting speeding automobile leaving golf club, presumably somewhere in Scotland; note kilted caddies. 31¼ins. × 27ins.:79.5cm × 69cm.

£60 — £100

566. Note apparent right-hand drive in this French Parisian oil painting, with three females from different walks of life endeavouring to secure a taxi, entitled 'Le Jugement de Paris' by Albert Guillaume. 34½ins. × 29½ins.:87.5cm × 75cm.

£700 — £900

567. An oil painting used as an original for a Delage advertisement and depicting Delage coupe de ville. Circa 1925.

£150 — £250

568. Produced in the early 1930s as decoration for a child's bedroom, a comic motoring frieze, the section shown depicting a head-on collision.

£100 — £150

569. A fine study in oils of a 'Blower' 4½ litre Bentley driven by Tim Birkin with W.O. Bentley acting as riding mechanic, entitled 'Tourist Trophy 1929' by Dion Pears, 24ins. × 36ins.:61cm × 91cm. Note supercharger between dumb-irons to front of car.

£300 — £400

570. A theatre poster advertising 'The Girl in the Taxi' at the Lyric Theatre, Shaftesbury Avenue. 1920s.

£50 — £60

571. Using a dramatic artist's impression, together with a photographic insert, this Castrol advertising board indicates Blue Bird's world land speed record at 245 m.p.h. The record was set at Daytona Beach, Florida, in February 1931.

£15 — £25

572. A popular pre-war brand of cigarette was Wills's 'Star'. Illustrated here, an advertising poster showing motor racing at Brooklands; the car in the foreground (in relief) is an ERA with Raymond Mays at the wheel. A dynamic poster. Circa 1935.

£70 — £100

573. Using a motoring theme and advertising '30 smiles to the gallon if it's Wm. Younger's'. Note thirty-one smiling faces in charabanc, presumably the driver was a happy tee-totaller? Circa 1930.

£10 — £15

Cigarette Cards, Postcards
Documents, Guides, Maps
Books and Periodicals

The dawn of popular motoring coincided with the Golden Age of British postcards, and a popular interpretation reflected in the comic manner the disasters which befell the early automobilist. In addition to these cards, the races of the day were captured in photographic form as were serious crashes, motor shows, etc. Later the postcard became useful as a manufacturer's promotional item.

Apart from an early set of cigarette cards produced by Lambert & Butler in 1908 and a few photographic cards by Ogden, it was not until the 'twenties that cigarette manufacturers drew on the motor car as a popular theme. From then until the 'thirties many colourful and informative sets were produced by various makers. Radiators, index marks, as well as styles of car are covered.

A vast number of books, either informative guides or autobiographies, were produced from early days, and collectors will seek out their own popular titles from their sphere of interest. The periodical was likewise in demand from the beginning, *The Autocar* being first produced in 1895. Since then a number of successful magazines on motoring and motor sport have followed and are widely enjoyed. Particularly interesting are some of the exciting cover illustrations from the 'thirties, notably *Speed* and the Motor Show numbers produced by *Autocar* and *Motor*.

574. Issued as part of an enormous series of cigarette cards, two Ogden's 'Tabs' series (photographic type), showing left, a 6 h.p. Daimler and right, The King's Auto Instructor. Circa 1903.

£2 — £3 each

575. A selection of five cigarette cards from Lambert & Butler's set of twenty-five issued in November 1908. Two types of back exist, green back as shown and a rarer plain back; various body styles are depicted.

£80 — £120 set

576. Fourteen years later, in October 1922, Lambert & Butler introduced another series of twenty-five cards, followed in June 1923 by a second series of twenty-five. In 1926 a series of fifty cards was introduced.

£12 — £15 set

577. Four cards from Lambert & Butler's scarce 'Motor Cars' — third series of fifty issued 1926, coloured cards with details on reverse.

£40 — £60 set

578. Produced in 1926 by Lambert & Butler, a useful and informative set of Motor Index Marks which allowed identification of registration letters to cities and regions. First four cards shown from a series of fifty.

£15 — £25 set

579. Still by Lambert & Butler, this series of twenty-five Motor Car Radiators was from a period when radiators gave instant identification of make. On coloured backgrounds, with distinctive features mentioned on reverse of cards. 1928.

£20 — £30 set

580. Another Lambert & Butler motor inspired set are these 'Hints & Tips for Motorists', again giving useful information on driving and maintaining the motor car, four from a series of twenty-five issued in 1929.

£10 — £15 set

581. A selection of cards from Lambert & Butler's 'How Motor Cars Work', issued June 1931 as a set of twenty-five. Informative diagrammatic cards.

£8 — £10 set

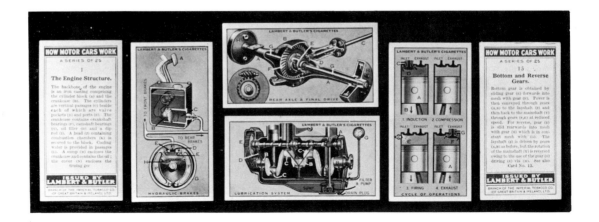

582. Produced for inclusion in the boys' comic, the *Triumph,* these cards are part of a series of thirty-two produced by Amalgamated Press Ltd. in 1932. The reverse shows index marks giving place of original registration.

£10 — £15 set

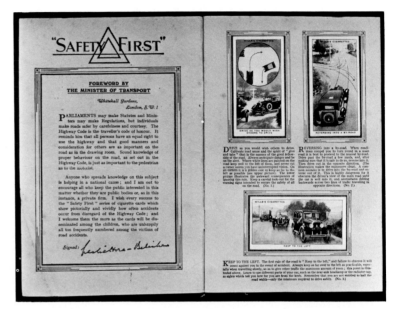

583. Here shown in their special album, the first three cards from Wills's 'Safety First' series issued in 1934. Note reference to Highway Code in foreword with facsimile signature of Hore-Belisha, Minister of Transport.

£4 — £6 set

584. Player's, like other cigarette companies, produced motoring cards; shown here are their 1936 series of fifty, and second series of fifty issued in May 1937. These Player's cards have adhesive backs and special albums were available at a penny each.

£5 — £8 set

585. An Edwardian novelty postcard, embossed and coloured. If instructions to lower left of card are followed, a horn-like sound is produced from an aperture in the lamp. Like many attractive cards of the period, this one was printed in Germany for British consumption.

£8 — £12

586. Produced on the Continent, a charming early 20th century postcard showing tiny tots enjoying the pleasures of the automobile. Circa 1905.

£2 — £3

587. Postcards issued as souvenirs of Prince Borghèse's win in the 'Pékin-Paris' race of 1907, driving a 24 h.p. Itala. Note below card commemorating vehicles encountering adverse weather.

£8 — £10 each

588. Together with facsimile signatures, Prince Borghèse and Luigi Barzini, standing by the Itala. Note Italian stamps affixed to front of card.

£8 — £10 each

589. Two advertising postcards. Left, monochrome 'Thornycroft' at the Olympia Motor Show 1905; below, coloured 'Ruston-Hornsby' card with specification and prices to reverse. 1921.

£4 — £6 each

590. Two interesting photographs. Left, Prince Olaf driving a miniature Cadillac in Pall Mall; and right, Panhard Levassor's stand at a Paris Motor Show, circa 1910.

£4 — £6 each

591. A comic greetings card incorporating motoring theme, the cover by Dudley Buxton, shown together with inside rhyme and greetings. Circa 1907.

£3 — £5

592. An attractive early advertising postcard extolling the merits of products of the Hanover Rubber Company. Circa 1911.

£8 — £10

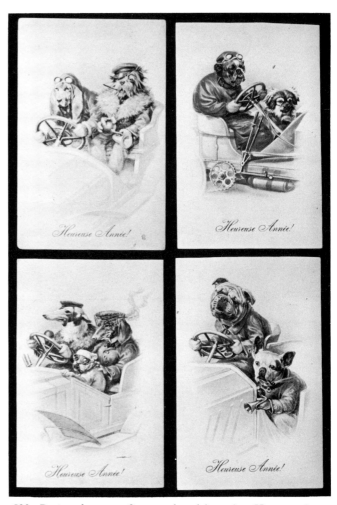

593. Postcards were often produced in series. Here are four finely illustrated French postcards with various breeds of dogs as drivers and passengers in automobiles. Circa 1910.

£8 — £12 each

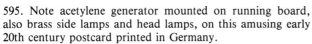

594. From the immediate pre-World War I period, an English postcard with dust-coated driver operating pump.
£2 — £3

595. Note acetylene generator mounted on running board, also brass side lamps and head lamps, on this amusing early 20th century postcard printed in Germany.
£1.50 — £2.50

596. Early postcards of automobiles are much sought after, here shown are two Italian limousines. Note the fine accessories, in the form of lamps, horn, etc.

£3 — £5 each

597. An amusing postcard relating to Henry Ford's early motor car, printed in England. Circa 1920.

£8 — £12

THERE was a little man;
His name was Henry Ford.
He took a bit of rubber
And a little bit of board,
A little drop of petrol
And an old tin can,
And shoved the lot together,
And the darned thing ran!

598. A French card showing military vehicle wreckage at Arras. Circa 1915.

£3 — £5

599. Collecting 'Accident and Disaster' cards can be a theme in itself for collectors. This French card depicts an automobile wreckage, the result of being hit by a train. Circa 1920.

£5 — £8

600. More than just a postcard — concealed beneath the lift-up flap, a pull-out strip of views of Southbourne, a popular south coast resort. The car is a Rolls-Royce Tourer. Circa 1920.

£2 — £3

601. Postcard size photographs are also of collectable interest, here a privately taken snapshot of a Rolls-Royce limousine with chauffeur at the wheel. Circa 1925.

£2 — £3

602. From the 1930s, a Mabel Lucie Attwell comic postcard, the car loosely based on a Riley Tourer. Note the AA badge and comic number plate.

£2 — £3

603. The *Motor* magazine produced a series of postcards of motor racing drivers. Top left, an advertising card, the other three cards are examples from the series of twelve. Note the advantages of bulk buying on quoted prices, monochrome. Late 1930s.

£2 — £4 each

604. Two later advertising postcards, produced by Esso, mention approval of use with Vauxhall and Morris cars. Mid-1930s.

£2 — £4 each

605. Produced as a series of monochrome postcards by Lewis Berger and Sons to advertise their 'Lifeguard Polish', these cards depict Hillman and Austin saloons showing mirror-like finish and giving extracts of letters from delighted customers. 1930s.

£2 — £3 each

606. A further series of Berger advertising postcards showing paint finish to various commercial vehicles. 1930s.

£1 — £2 each

607. Early driving licence, issued by the County Borough of Eastbourne for twelve months from August 1913. Not renewed, possibly the owner volunteered for service at the outbreak of World War I, a fortnight before the licence was due to expire.

£4 — £6

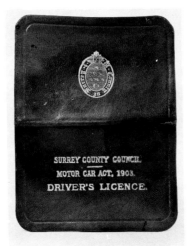

608. Another early driver's licence, issued by the County of Surrey, note county crest to reverse. Leather covered, embossed gold lettering. Also shown open, giving details of licence, issued for one year only. Circa 1912.

£4 — £6

609. A selection of drivers' licences covering the period January 1907 to August 1966. All issued to the same driver (over fifty-nine years' motoring). Also a tax disc for a Morris Cowley covering the quarter from October to December 1933. Licences, from left to right, 1930-31, 1907-8, 1926-29, 1920-30, 1929-30, 1931-36, 1936-66.

£25 — £40 set

Colour Plate 28. Illustrated by Charles Crombie for Perrier, eleven postcards entitled MOTORITIS (presumably from a set of twelve), and depicting humorous motor incidents relating to various road traffic acts. Circa 1905.

£5 — £8 each

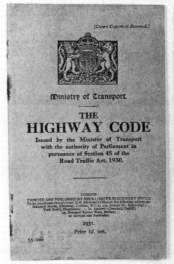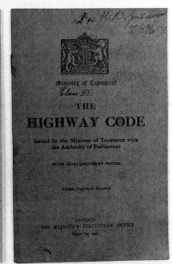

610. For external use, nearside mounted, a typical tax disc holder, 1930s and '40s. It is interesting to note that the vehicle mentioned on the disc was exempt from duty, presumably due to war service.

£3 — £5

611. The First Edition of the Highway Code issued by the Ministry of Transport in 1931, price 1d., shown beside a 1935 edition with supplementary notes.

£3 — £5 first edition

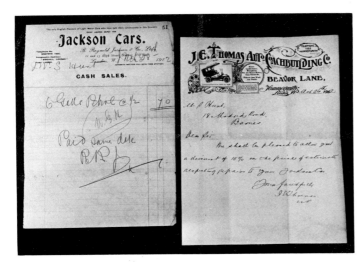

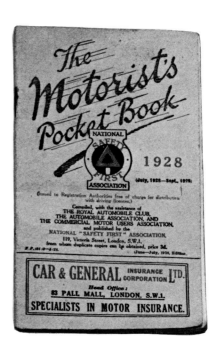

612. Two early motor company letter headings. Left, Jackson Cars petrol receipt for 1912, note 7s. (35p) purchased six gallons! Right, attractively headed letter from J.E. Thomas Auto-Coachbuilding Co., offering a 10% discount for repairs to a Jackson Car, 1912.

£1.50 — £2.50 each

613. *The Motorist's Pocket Book,* July-Sept. 1928, was produced by the National Safety First Association and was issued to Registration Authorities free of charge for distribution with driving licences. Useful hints and general information.

£2 — £3

Colour Plate 29. A group of five early 20th century colour postcards, various types, English and Continental, circa 1904-6.

£5 — £8 each

Colour Plate 30. Four Italian postcards with motor racing connections including racing calendar, advertising events, etc. Circa 1925-31.

£5 — £8 each

614. This pre-war *Air Raid Precautions Manual,* 1938, was a public service publication issued to employees of London Transport.

£1 — £2

615. Probably remembered foremost for his series of World War II propaganda posters, 'Careless Talk Costs Lives', the cartoonist Fougasse produced these drawings for an amusing 'safe driving' booklet presented to drivers by the Royal Society for the Prevention of Accidents in 1947.

£1 — £2

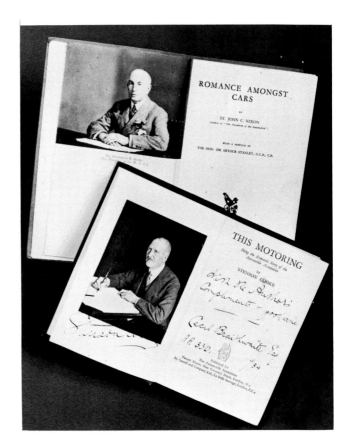

616. Two interesting books published in the 1930s, recalling the development of the R.A.C. and A.A. respectively. Above, St. John C. Nixon's *Romance Amongst Cars;* below, *This Motoring* by Stenson Cooke with author's signature and inscription.

£10 — £15 Nixon   £1 — £2 Cooke

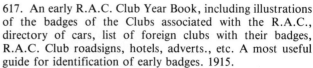

617. An early R.A.C. Club Year Book, including illustrations of the badges of the Clubs associated with the R.A.C., directory of cars, list of foreign clubs with their badges, R.A.C. Club roadsigns, hotels, adverts., etc. A most useful guide for identification of early badges. 1915.

£8 — £12

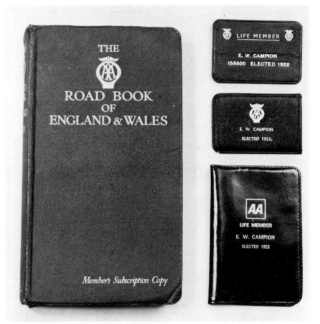

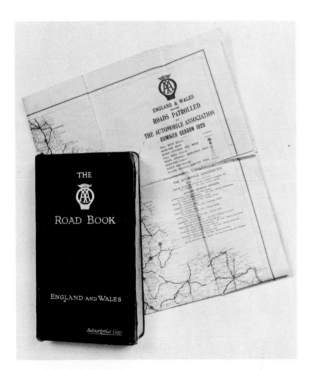

618. A Member's Subscription Copy of the A.A. Road Book (2nd edition); a scarce A.A. life member's membership card of green leather with gold lettering issued in 1922, the reverse bearing A.A. address and Secretary Sir Stenson Cooke; an A.A. life member's leather card holder, and a more recent A.A. life member's wallet. The life member referred to, E.W. Campion, owned a 12.9 h.p. Rover four seat open tourer number XK 199 at time of election, 1922.

£20 — £30 set

619. Showing folding map (enclosed in interior flap) an A.A. Subscription Copy Road Book, blue cloth with gilt lettering. 1925.

£2 — £4

620. Two examples of A.A. members' handbooks — a 1935-36 edition which, apart from giving the usual information, also includes a car tax table from a period when tax was calculated on h.p., usually 15s. per additional h.p. Also shown, the first post-war member's handbook, 1949-50.

£1 — £2

The Mascot.

Colour Plate 31. A wonderfully humorous postcard entitled 'The Mascot' depicting smiling lucky black cat radiator mascot and scowling partly-submerged motorist. Circa 1920.
£8 — £12

Colour Plate 32. The cover of the popular 'thirties periodical *Speed* certainly endeavoured to give expression to the title. These contain many thrilling accounts of events at Brooklands and other race circuits, record breaking attempts, etc., a real insight to the period they record, issues shown circa 1935-37.
£5 — £8 each
£300 complete run

621. This A.A. booklet included an application for membership form and various illustrations of A.A. services, etc. 1930s.

£1 — £2

622. The R.A.C. and the A.A. provided suggested route itineraries; here shown an R.A.C. example prepared for a journey from Brighton to Bristol, all kinds of useful tips and hints included. Also shown, official R.A.C. Town Plans to be used with itinerary. Circa 1930.

£1 — £2 each

623. From the days of varying town speed limits, an extract from a large linen backed wall map. These limits were shown on entry to town or village by a sign employing a plate displaying speed superimposed on a white circle. Horsham must have been rather confusing for the day tripper with both 5 and 10 m.p.h. limits. Circa 1914.

£8 — £12

624. A useful early guide to the motorist, *The Car* road book and guide shown here with map, note compass inset to cover, hotel details, etc. 1908-09.

£15 — £25

625. Specially produced for the motorist, this map of England divides into three parts, and was ingenious in that folds allowed any area to be viewed whilst preserving the book-like form. Shown here with its original leather covered box.

£25 — £40

626. A Packard map case with twenty-four sections, a practical promotional gift. 1920s.

£12 — £18

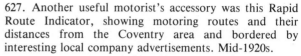

627. Another useful motorist's accessory was this Rapid Route Indicator, showing motoring routes and their distances from the Coventry area and bordered by interesting local company advertisements. Mid-1920s.
£1 — £2

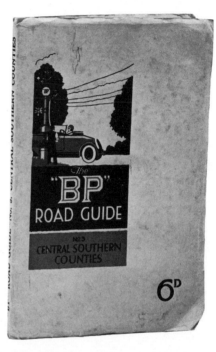

628. Petrol companies also produced motorists' guides, presumably as a service to motorists and a method of promoting petrol sales. Shown here, a pre-war guide No. 3, giving list of B.P. petrol pumps, places of interest, etc.
£1 — £2

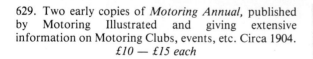

629. Two early copies of *Motoring Annual,* published by Motoring Illustrated and giving extensive information on Motoring Clubs, events, etc. Circa 1904.
£10 — £15 each

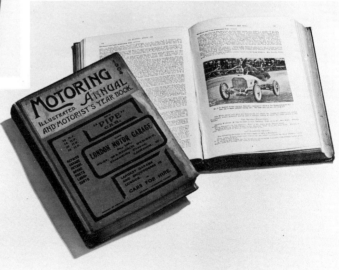

630. A page from Cooper's Coachbuilders' Art Journal Diary for 1908, advertisements, diary, specifications, tables, etc. Note electric cigar lighter not as recent an accessory as may have been thought.
£5 — £8

631. Three books published in the mid-1920s covering bodywork including, left to right, design and construction, body drawing and coach painting. Well produced books of specific contemporary interest.
£100 — £200
£100 — £150 with companion portfolio
£80 — £120

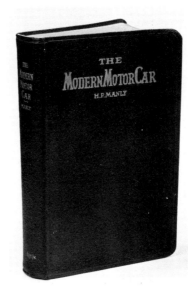

Left: 632. *The Modern Motor Car* by H.P. Manly, mainly relating to general upkeep of the motor car. Circa 1919.
£10 — £12

Right: 633. An Italian driving instruction book by G. Pedretti, published in Milan 1930.
£5 — £8

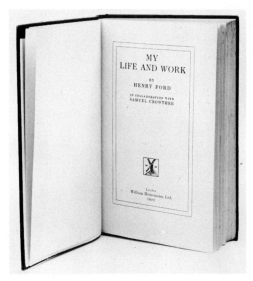

634. An instigator of mass production and a legend in his own lifetime, Henry Ford's autobiography *My Life and Work,* published by Heinemann in 1923.

£7 — £10

635. A German book on automobiles and motor sport with a startling cover illustration in green and black. Written by von Richard Hofmann. Circa 1926.

£75 — £100

636. With a powerful dust-jacket illustration by Roland Davies *Combat,* a motor racing history, was written by Barré Lyndon, first edition published 1933. It should be remembered that dust-jackets are vulnerable but important value-wise for their illustrations.

£20 — £30

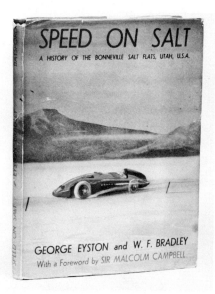

637. Famed for his distance records, George Eyston, later driver of the Thunderbolt record car, wrote *Speed on Salt,* a history of the Bonneville salt flats, together with W.F. Bradley, in 1936.

£5 — £8

638. Although all early motoring magazines are collectable, those recording motor shows are particularly desirable, since they contain prices and specifications of the coming year's cars. Here shown *The Motor* for Tuesday, October 19th 1926, Second Show Number.

£12 — £20

639. *The Motor* produced these useful price lists of cars, which were reprinted from the magazine and issued free by the Editor, differing formats, prices and specifications. Circa 1925-1936.

£4 — £6 each

640. Two copies of *The Motor* publicity brochures giving reviews for years 1928 and 1929, published by Temple Press with illustrations by Bryan De Grineau.

£10 — £15

641. The development of *The Cyclecar* magazine into the *Light Car* magazine is illustrated through these three copies. Left, No. 1 27th November 1912, centre *The Light Car & Cyclecar* January 1918, and right a Motor Show issue for October 1937.

£2 — £3 each

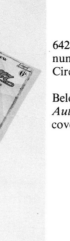

642. A selection of *The Autocar* magazine, all show numbers. Venues include Earls Court and Olympia. Circa 1927-36.

£8 — £12 each

Below, bound (not by the publisher) volumes of *The Autocar* for 1939 complete with advertisements and covers. Of greater value than those bound without.

£80 — £100 year

643. The Riley Motor Club produced this monthly magazine, *The Riley Record,* the example shown giving an illustrated review of 1935 events.

£2 — £3

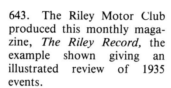

644. Car owners' clubs produced their own journals, here a copy of *Bugantics,* the Bugatti owners' club magazine, for July 1935.

£25 — £35

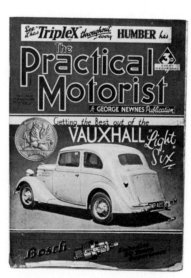

645. Various manufacturers produced their own magazine, shown here two copies of *The Vauxhall Motorist.* Note clever artwork on domed headlamp. Original price 4d. Circa 1936.

£1.50 — £2.50

646. Introduced during the 1930s, *The Practical Motorist* contained hints, tips and articles for the do-it-yourself motorist.

£1 each

Trophies, Programmes and Competition Motoring

The competitive spirit of early motorists soon found its place in rallies and races with inevitable prizes for the winners. Some of these are very elaborate trophies, their value enhanced by the presence of the original inscription which has sometimes been buffed out for re-use; many of the large silver trophies have been scrapped for their bullion content. The uniqueness of most major trophies makes pricing difficult, background research, etc. playing a factor in ultimately determining value.

If you could not win a trophy, you could at least bring home a programme of the event and here again is a colourful and informative area. In this country, from the advent of its birth in 1907 to the outbreak of the Second World War, the Brooklands motor racing course regularly held competitions. Brooklands programmes include details of entrants and their cars, provisions for scoring laps, advertising, etc.

647. An early silver-gilt Brooklands cup for the May Handicap won by Percy Lambert 'on 19.6 Austin' (Pearley III). This famous early racing driver held many Brooklands lap and distance records; he was killed during an attempt on the One Hour record at Brooklands in 1913.

£800 — £1,200

648. An Essex Motor Club plaque to competitor B. Eyston for Brooklands six hours Endurance Race 1927, mounted on ebonised base.

£40 — £50

Colour Plate 33. A selection of Brooklands racing programmes, five showing different covers for special events circa 1934-35; top right, normal cover.

£5 — £10 each

Colour Plate 34. A further selection of Brooklands Official Race Cards (Programmes). Note colour change effect on three of similar design.

£5 — £10 each

649. Rewarding a sixth place in the 1926 Brooklands 200 Miles Race, this Junior Car Club bronze plaque depicts two racing cars on banking, speeding towards figure of Victory; in presentation case.

£15 — £20

650. An Austrian Motor Trophy in Continental silver, inscribed FAHRT UM DEN OSTERREICHISCHEN ALPEN-POKAL 14-17 JUNI 1930 and having eight Austrian motor club badges suspended from lip of stem. 10¾ins.:27cm high.

£70 — £80

651. The British Racing Drivers' Club 500 Miles Race B.A.R.C. silver Tankard won by J.D. Benjafield in October 1930 in a supercharged 4½ litre Bentley, for fastest lap speed of 122.97 m.p.h. Benjafield came second overall at an average speed of 112.12 m.p.h., the fastest average in the race.

£600 — £800

652. This bronze trophy, in the form of an M.G. Midget racing car, was produced to commemorate George Eyston's record speed on Pendine Sands, February 1932, on oak base with brass plaque. 10ins.:25.5cm wide. Sold for £380 by Sotheby's Belgravia on 25th April, 1980.

653. A similar bronze figure of an Amazon with Javelin by A. Bouraine was illustrated in the Crystal Palace programme for 24th April 1937, as the Coronation Trophy and presented by Jack Barclay Ltd.
£500 — £800

654. An important and impressive Le Mans twenty-four hour race trophy 'Index of Performance', won by Chinetti and Lord Selsdon in 1949 driving a 2 litre V12 Ferrari (the first Le Mans twenty-four hour race since 1939). They won the race outright as well as 'Index of Performance', Chinetti having won already in 1932 and 1934. The trophy, of patinated bronze with octagonal cup-bearing tablet, depicts motor racing scenes in high relief, the square central column with figures of Victory being supported on a square marble base, with presentation inscription.
£800 — £1,200

Colour Plate 35. A tinplate model of a contender for the world land speed record in the 1930s, and scarcer than other similar toys in that the original car was unsuccessful. Made by Günthermann (unmarked, except 'foreign') with clockwork motor handbrake, applied flats and pressed wheels and tyres. 22ins.:56cm long. See also no. 734, p. 227.

Colour Plate 36. Note centrally mounted headlamp on this hand enamelled Bing De Dion Bouton, tinplate and clockwork. Circa 1905. See also no. 713, p. 221.
£750 — £1,000

655. An attractive Edwardian silver presentation medallion, 1½ins.:4cm diameter. Obverse with four seater tourer, reverse with wreath and space for presentation inscription, hallmark date for Birmingham 1907.
£25 — £35

656. Incorporating a flaming torch and winged wheel, this bronze motoring medallion was issued by Paix & Cie. French, circa 1925.
£5 — £8

657. Four gold Motor Cycling Club medals for the London to Edinburgh Rally circa mid-1920s, note 1924 for cycle car and 1926 for car.
£50 — £70

Colour Plate 37. Caught speeding! The German company Marklin produced a high quality constructional car. This limousine, loosely based on a Horch, has leaf springs with shackles, universally jointed propeller shaft, working steering, opening driver's door and handbrake. Known as the 1101 series. 15ins.:38cm long, mid-1930s. (Note driver is from a No. 2 Mecanno constructor car, policeman of unknown origin.) See also no. 744, p. 230.

658. A scarce programme for the Tourist Trophy and '1,500' Trophy Races in the Isle of Man, circa 1921, issued by Talbot-Darracq, and giving details of drivers and cars.

£20 — £25

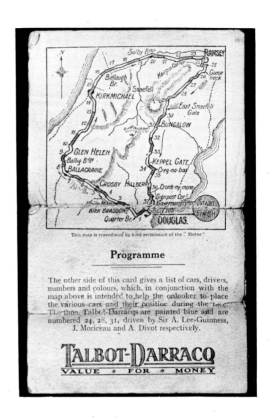

659. Brooklands Year Books 1930-34, with interesting information relating to the track and membership of B.A.R.C. Note change in badge for 1932, and 1933 introducing Aero Club badge.

£15 — £25 each

660. Programmes provide an interesting area for the collector; an official programme for the R.A.C. International Tourist Trophy Race at Belfast in 1929. Note advertisement for *The Motor* giving race report.

£15 — £20

661. Three Brooklands programmes. Left, International Trophy Race organised by Junior Car Club; centre, a scarce Emergency Edition with plain black and white cover, called 'Race Card'; right, '200 Miles Race' organised by Junior Car Club on August 27th 1938.

£5 — £10 each

662. Four Brooklands programmes including, top, '500 Miles Race', organised by British Racing Drivers' Club 19th September 1936, 'Dunlop International Car Race' September 24th 1938; below, 'International Trophy Race' organised by Junior Car Club May 7th 1938, and British Racing Drivers' Club Brooklands meeting, September 17th 1938.

£5 — £10 each

663. In addition to Brooklands, other racing circuits held regular events; shown here, two Crystal Palace programmes, one a composite meeting for cars and motorcycles, the other a race for cars; and a Southport Motor Racing Club programme for 5th September 1936.

£5 — £10 each

664. A photograph of three famous E.R.A. racing cars on part of the Campbell circuit was used as the cover for this souvenir brochure of Brooklands 1938, which is filled with interesting articles and advertisements.

£8 — £12

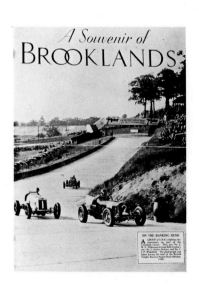

665. From an album of photographs mainly relating to Brooklands, two shots of the Two Hundred Mile Race, 1923 and two of a 1914 8 h.p. Mathis in the paddock at Brooklands, 1920.

£80 — £120

666. For historians of world record attempts, an interesting letter from Malcolm Campbell to The Hon. Mrs. Lort Phillips, dated 22.9.24, mentioning his forthcoming record attempt on Pendine Sands. 'I have come down to attack world's records with my big car ... I shall be going out for the records on Wednesday next.' Campbell broke the World Land Speed record at 146.16 m.p.h. (an improvement of 0.15 m.p.h. over the previous record). In the book, *The Record Breakers* by Leo Villa and Tony Gray, reference is made to the fact that Campbell 'sent for the R.A.C. officials and told them ... that he wasn't going to make an attempt on the record, but he wanted them there to time his speed. Then, without any fuss or warning, he put his foot down ...' This letter appears to imply a pre-determined intention!

£40 — £60

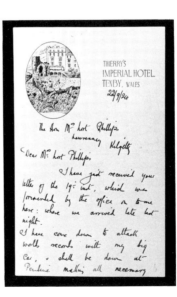

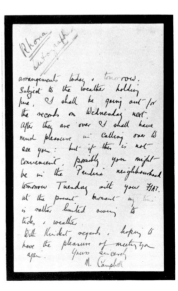

Motoring Novelties

As well as their standard advertising motoring companies, particularly in the 'thirties, produced many cheap but useful gifts for promotional purposes, either for retailers or retailers' clients. These normally took the form of ashtrays, etc. and can provide an interesting but distant side of motoring collectables.

Not all items were given away but could be purchased reasonably, for example crested china vehicles of the Goss type. However, these should not be confused with the wider contemporary novelties that used the attractions of motoring to sell other products, e.g. teapots, and smoking requisites, games, etc.

667. This presentation silver cigarette box has a realistic early period racing car in relief mounted on exposed cedarwood lined box. Circa 1906.

£60 — £100

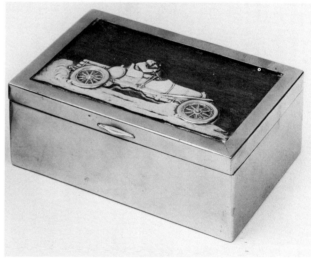

668. A smoker's companion in the form of a veteran car, wood with plated metal fittings and faceted glass to lamps, rubber tyres, seating section removable for cigarettes, etc. Circa 1910.

£50 — £75

669. A cigarette box incorporating dispenser based on a 1930s saloon, the dispensed cigarette appears next to running board.

£20 — £30

670. An interesting pre-World War I ceramic ashtray with artillery type wheel as centre.

£15 — £25

671. An attractive embossed copper ashtray promoting Daimler motor cars and depicting an Edwardian model. Circa 1910.

£10 — £15

672. Manufactured by W. Miller & Co., Birmingham, who produced promotional ashtrays for various companies, this copper version has attractive transferred ceramic centre for Morris Commercial Cars. 1920s.

£5 — £8

673. Although many motor factories, companies, etc. produced give-away ashtrays, this copper ashtray with enamelled centre in the form of a speedometer was produced by A.T. Speedometer Co. Ltd. and has enhanced interest value as A.T. produced speedometers for Rolls-Royce, Bentley and other notable makers. 1930s.

£5 — £8

674. A 1930s ashtray incorporating small size A.A. member's badge, note voided section beneath, where number and detail are normally placed.

£5 — £8

675. Well known in the 1930s as motor factors, the firm of G.T. Riches produced this brass advertising ashtray, note 'ORNO' trademark beneath Riches' emblem. 1930s.

£5 — £8

676. An embossed triangular brass ashtray with Peugeot 'Lion' motif, 1930s.

£5 — £8

677. Using the Vauxhall 'V' and flutes to advantage, this chromium plated base metal ashtray also incorporated a miniature version of the 1930s type mascot.

£5 — £8

678. A popular advertising idea came in the form of 'Tyre' ashtrays, this 'India Balloon' 600 × 19 is typical. 5ins.:12.5cm diameter. Circa 1930.

£3 — £5

679. Above average quality, this India ashtray advertises their 'Super Nonskid' 600 × 18 tyre and incorporates India's red band to tyre wall, removable bakelite centre with raised 'Britannia' motif. 5¼ins.:13.5cm diameter.

£3 — £5

680. A Goodyear Eagle tyre ashtray, glass centre, 5¾ins.:14.5cm diameter. Circa 1940.

£3 — £5

681. A post-war Goodyear tyre ashtray having late pattern tread. Note Goodyear Eagle to side.

£2 — £3

683. A fine Continental desk inkwell in the form of an early racing car, note opening bonnet and boot, signed 'W. Furick'. 15ins.:38cm long. Circa 1912.

£150 — £250

682. A dashboard mounted cigarette dispenser, chromium plated, German manufacture. 'Thirties.

£3 — £5

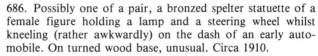

684. An attractive paper menu holder in the form of a veteran car, the details of menu on roof canopy. Number plate marked Hotel Metropole, Brighton, and dated 1905.

£30 — £50

685. In the form of a Bugatti radiator, this is in fact a trophy with later red enamel badge to top. Later such items were made as spirit flasks. 7½ins.:19cm high.

£30 — £50

686. Possibly one of a pair, a bronzed spelter statuette of a female figure holding a lamp and a steering wheel whilst kneeling (rather awkwardly) on the dash of an early automobile. On turned wood base, unusual. Circa 1910.

£15 — £20

687. Advertising an insurance agency of the Motor Union Co. Ltd. and A.A. motor policies, a metal framed glass lampshade produced for office use. 7ins.:18cm high. 1930s.
£20 — £30

688. Produced to carry motor documents and insurance papers, this aluminium container was presumably given by the Red Cross Motor Policy. Note written-on registration number and make. 1930s.
£3 — £5

689. An attractive presentation plaque commemorating twenty-five years' association with the Austin Motor Company, silvered white metal with Austin emblem.
£12 — £18

690. Again Austin, these plated napkin rings were possibly intended as gifts to customers, garage proprietors, etc. 1930s.
£8 — £12

691. A 'give-away' paper knife, the handle with raised decoration in the form of open tourer and figure of Victory. Art Nouveau. Circa 1912.
£8 — £12

692. This yardstick employing the motto 'Service — every inch of the way' was given by Kettle's of Maidstone, a promotional gift.
£3 — £5

693. For use in the car, this clothes brush was a gift from 'G. Ashton, York & Albion Garages', note imitation tortoiseshell backing and white metal rim. 1930s.
£2 — £3

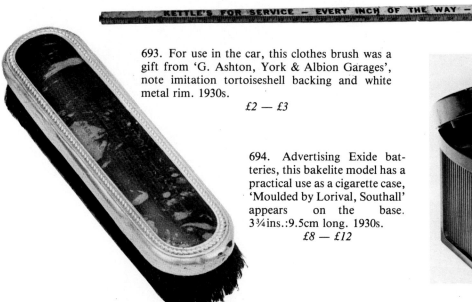

694. Advertising Exide batteries, this bakelite model has a practical use as a cigarette case, 'Moulded by Lorival, Southall' appears on the base. 3¾ins.:9.5cm long. 1930s.
£8 — £12

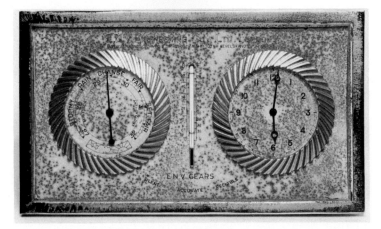

695. Not from a motor car but for desk use, this combination shows barometer, thermometer and clock, produced for E.N.V. Engineering for presentation to distributors. 10½ins.:26.5cm wide. Note crown wheel bezels. 1930s.
£25 — £40

696. A promotional gift, this Vauxhall desk blotter of white moulded plastic bearing enamelled Vauxhall badge is shown here with its original box. 1930s.
£5 — £8

697. In the form of a torque-wrench, this tie clip was probably a give-away item from the manufacturers. 1930s.

£1 — £2

698. Three give-away advertising products. Right, a Shell Mex tie pin, 1930s; top right, a Castrol lapel badge in green and red enamel with pin back, 1930s; bottom right, from a range of give-away items, an Austin penknife.

£1 — £3 each

699. A silver-plated pocket watch, the case decorated with an early chain driven racing car, the face advertising Saucer sparking plugs. Circa 1908.

£150 — £250

700. Not a toy, but probably produced for promotional purposes, a large and heavy die-cast 1,000 h.p. Sunbeam record car with driver and details of record. Note 'Dunlop' tyres. Generally poor condition, but still impressive. 27½ins.:70cm long. Circa 1928.

£100 — £150

701. The board and playing pieces for the new 'Motor Race' Game, a snakes and ladders type entertainment with gains and hazards encountered on the throw of the dice, c.1915.
£15 — £25

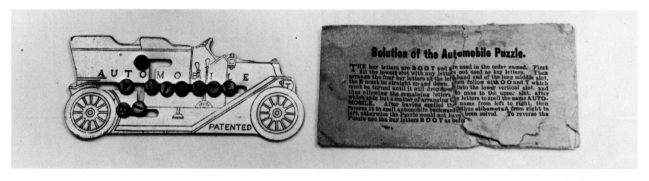

702. From the Edwardian period, an entertaining Automobile puzzle in the form of a nickel plated car with sliding letters, complete with original packet bearing instructions. 4ins.:10cm long.
£10 — £15

703. Produced by the publishers George Newnes, a Tit-Bits Teaser No. 4 comprising fourteen wooden blocks, each with a vehicle name. A very difficult puzzle indeed, we've tried it! Circa 1930.
£3 — £5

704. A very colourful Esso promotional game featuring Brooklands track with press-out cardboard cars and dice, looks fun to play! 1930s.

£15 — £20

705. Another oil company's promotional gimmick, this Filtrate Oils disc can be turned through various cartoon sections in an endeavour to garage car, amusing. 5½ins.:14cm diameter.

£1 — £2

706. This unusual Shell promotional idea, with Winter and Summer views, endeavours to achieve a three dimensional effect through window viewer — sides include slogan 'Be up to date, Shellubricate'. Colourful and imaginative. Two illustrations shown to convey effect. Early 1930s.

£5 — £8

707. An attractive and scarce crest china racing car made by Crown, Devon, and bearing arms of Douglas, Isle of Man. Tail marked 'Manx International Motor Car Race'. Note riding mechanic and Brooklands fishtail exhaust. 5¾ins.:14.5cm long. 1920s.

£50 — £60

708. Again a suitable collecting area in its own right, china vehicles enjoyed a period of popularity from the 1920s to 1940s. Here shown a four seater touring car loosely based on Vauxhall design, finished white overall. 5¼ins.:13.5cm long.

£10 — £15

709. Many china cars are to be found in the form of teapots, here using driver's head and tonneau as lid, crazed glaze finish overall. 1930s.

£25 — £40

710. Another 1930s novelty teapot in the form of a single seater open car with driver's head acting as a knob to the lid.

£25 — £40

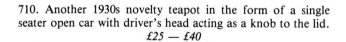

Toys and Pedal Cars

As an extension to the interest in the full size automobile, many collectors like to possess a contemporary toy of their vehicle. However, many manufacturers' products are only loosely based on a real car. By the mid-'thirties Dinky Toys were becoming popular and many of their models were recognisable and in fact identified in their catalogues, e.g. the 30 series of 1935 were the first cars to be given names — prior to this only body styles were mentioned. As an alternative to diecast toys, the collector may prefer tinplate and clockwork; normally of larger size, these were produced by the leading makers, particularly from Germany, France and Great Britain. The car manufacturer Citroën also produced some excellent tinplate toys, being representations of range.

Though not resembling any particular models, a number of novelty vehicles exist which may be ingenious and entertaining from the historical viewpoint. Toy Record Cars of the 'twenties and 'thirties are normally attractive and desirable.

For those preferring even larger models, a fine range of pedal cars exists, again some accurate representations and others pure fantasy.

711. Just as steam was used in certain veteran cars, notably the Stanley, it was also used to power certain early tinplate toy automobiles as an alternative to clockwork; here shown a rare Bing 'Spider' having spring front axle, headlamps, upholstered seats, finely spoked wheels with rubber tyres, hand enamelled. 9ins.:23cm long. Circa 1900.

£2,000 — £4,000

712. The name Gordon Bennet, synonymous with pioneer motor racing, is to be found on the bonnet of this early 20th century tinplate toy racing car by Günthermann. The driver is crouched in determined pose behind steering wheel, mechanic missing. German, a stylish and scarce toy. 8¼ins.:21cm long. Circa 1905.

£650 — £850

713. Based on the De Dion Bouton, an early hand enamelled tinplate and clockwork Bing two-seater automobile, lever operated brake, set steering, artillery type wheels with rubber tyres, pressed imitation leather deep buttoned upholstery and brass centrally mounted headlamp. View below shows G.B.N. (Gre Bing Nuremberg) trademark to rear. Circa 1906. See also Colour Plate 36, p. 204.

£800 — £1,000

714. Using a similar chassis to the previous item, this Bing tinplate two-seater represents a Mercedes model; finished in original dark green, lined in yellow with pink upholstery. 9½ins.:24cm long. Circa 1910.

£700 — £900

715. Capturing the Edwardian period, a fine tinplate and clockwork limousine by Carette, well detailed with luggage rack, uniformed chauffeur, lever operated brake. Finished in dark green with red details, lined in black and gilt. A classic toy. 15¾ins.:40cm long. Circa 1910.

£900 — £1,200

Colour Plate 38. Advertised in Gamages' 1911 catalogue as a hill climbing car, this Hessmobile fly-wheel driven racing car has driver in period racing attire and adopting a determined pose, bonnet removable to expose motor. See also no. 716.

Colour Plate 39. A classic toy of a classic car, J.E.P.'s Hispano Suiza open tourer, having sprung front bumper, gear box, operating steering, electric lights, treaded tyres and windscreen, 20½ins.:52cm long. The same manufacturer also produced a Rolls-Royce version. Circa 1928. See also no. 726, p. 225.

Colour Plate 40. This very realistic model of a Citroën 5cv Clover Leaf tourer was produced by Citroën themselves in 1923, clockwork mechanism operating steering, windscreen missing, c.1928. See also no. 727, p. 225.

716. Advertised by Gamages in 1911 as a hill climbing toy, this flywheel driven Hess racing car operates through winding of realistic starting handle, bonnet detachable to reveal mechanism. Driver clad realistically in period motoring clothing, printed detail, originally two flags were fitted to radiator, price in 1911 1s. 9d. (8½p). 8¾ins.:22cm long. See also Colour Plate 38.

£200 — £300

717. For the public service vehicle enthusiast, the taxi forms the most practical area for collecting, here shown a German made tinplate and clockwork model by H. Fischer of Nuremberg incorporating folding canopy, three hinged side doors, meter and hire sign to nearside, opera lamps. Head lamp and klaxon missing. Circa 1914.

£450 — £600

718. Just before World War I Bing produced this open tinplate and clockwork touring car, finished in navy blue, lined in yellow with grey interior, red seats and glass windscreen. Side mounted lamps are missing.

£350 — £450

719. A good representation of a Ford model T coupé constructed from lightweight tinplate with clockwork mechanism. Naturally finished in black, the manufacturer's trademark appears on number plate. 6¼ins.:16cm long. Bing, circa 1920.

£120 — £180

720. From the 1920s, this steam powered tinplate open touring car by Doll & Co. is shown with bonnet open to reveal boiler. Artillery type wheels with rubber tyres, operating clutch and steering, and three opening doors.
£900 — £1,200

721. Again from the 'twenties and by Bing, this limousine is powered by a two-speed clockwork motor, gear lever mounted to exterior with operating brake lever. Opening rear doors and glazed windscreen, rubber tyres, pillar mounted side lamps and chauffeur. Finished in cherry red and black with yellow lining. 15¼ins.:38.8cm long.
£500 — £700

722. This Voisin tourer by J.E.P. (French toymaker) has operating gear lever, well detailed klaxon, headlamps, etc. and is finished in blue with navy lining. Late 1920s.
£350 — £450

723. From the same maker, this Delage limousine uses the same tinplate chassis as the previous model. Finished in maroon with grey, black and scarlet details, here shown with original box. Circa 1930.
£450 — £600

724. Another J.E.P. tinplate saloon, this time a Panhard Levassor similar to previous model apart from radiator and louvres to bonnet. Finished in light brown, black and grey with scarlet lining (spot lamp missing, note klaxon). 13ins.:33cm long. Circa 1930.

£300 — £400

725. Unmistakably Renault by bonnet design, this J.E.P. tin-plate and clockwork saloon is well appointed having spotlight, klaxon, etc. Mechanism wound from starting handle position driving propeller shaft to back axle. Finished in olive green with black and gilt. 13½ins.:34cm long. Circa 1930.

£350 — £500

726. A road view of the Hispano Suiza shown in Colour Plate 39, illustrating transmission, steering, sprung bumper, etc., some restoration evident to running board and mudguard. Note number plate incorporates manufacturer's initials. See also Colour Plate 39, p. 222.

£800 — £1,200

727. The road view of the Citroën 5cv Clover Leaf tourer, seen in Colour Plate 40, p. 222, showing simplicity of the mechanism, steering and brakes; the mainspring is missing. Note André Citroën's trademark.

£350 — £450

728. Note open bonnet revealing stylised six cylinder engine. External gear lever with 'neutral − in gear', pressed tin wheels and tyres marked 'Semperit cord 31 × 4'. 9½ins.:24cm long. Moko, circa 1920.
£150 — £200

729. Advertised by Gamages in 1926 and described as 'Grand Prix of Europe 1924/25 World's Championship', this C.I.J. tinplate and clockwork P2 Alfa Romeo racing car is a large and impressive toy. This early model is finished in blue (French racing colour). Note presence of André dampers, brake drums and smooth balloon tyres. Shown with original box, price in 1926 25s. (£1.25). 20ins.:50.8cm long. See also Colour Plate 41, p. 239.
£500 — £700 mint examples

730. This later P2, circa 1929, is finished in silver (German racing colour) and has treaded tyres but no brake drums, dampers or starting handle, although the price has slumped to 35s. (£1.75). Manufacturer and size as above. See also Colour Plate 41, p. 239.
£500 — £700 mint examples

731. From the Kingsbury company (U.S.A.), this model of Malcolm Campbell's Bluebird record car came with cunningly hidden key. The company was responsible for making other record cars including The Golden Arrow and the 1,000 h.p. Sunbeam. Late 1920s.

£150 — £250

732. Also by Kingsbury, their version of Golden Arrow (compare with Günthermann product in 735). Note, the choice of the name 'Golden Arrow' may have been influenced by the cylinder configuration of the Napier Lion engine (arrowhead form).

£120 — £180

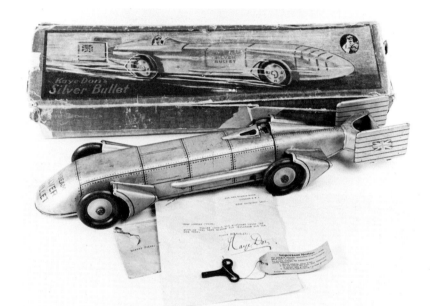

733. Of great interest due to the accompanying letter signed by Kaye Don (driver of the real Silver Bullet car) to a Master Price, asking him to accept the car as a Christmas gift and dated 22 December 1930 (the year of the record attempt). Note the variation to nose cowl with Silver Bullet in no. 734.

200 — £300

734. Above, a Kingsbury Sunbeam record car (driver missing). Finished in red with transferred flags. Right, a tinplate model of a contender for the world land speed record in the 1930s, and scarcer than other similar toys in that the original car was unsuccessful. Made by Günthermann (unmarked, except 'foreign') with clockwork motor handbrake, applied flags and pressed wheels and tyres. 22ins.:56cm long. See also Colour Plate 35, p. 204.

£100 — £150 Sunbeam   *£180 — £220 Silver Bullet*

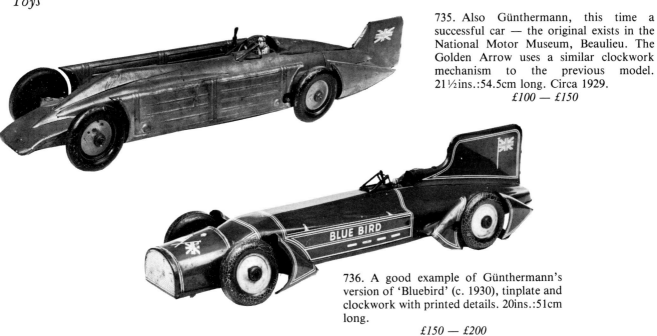

735. Also Günthermann, this time a successful car — the original exists in the National Motor Museum, Beaulieu. The Golden Arrow uses a similar clockwork mechanism to the previous model. 21½ins.:54.5cm long. Circa 1929.

£100 — £150

736. A good example of Günthermann's version of 'Bluebird' (c. 1930), tinplate and clockwork with printed details. 20ins.:51cm long.

£150 — £200

737. A British made Bluebird record car, tinplate and clockwork, with applied flags. Note facsimile signature of Malcolm Campbell (just visible in front of driver).

£50 — £80

738. Produced by Meccano (known for tinplate constructional toys), a No. 1 motor car constructor kit, built as a coupé. Also shown, a two-seater sports car. Alternative bodies available in kit utilising common chassis.

£100 — £150

739. The larger Meccano motor car constructor kit is known as the No. 2. Shown here an example which includes electric lights (available as an extra). Bodies, mudguards and radiators were interchangeable on a common chassis with short or long wheelbase options. Various colour combinations encountered. 13ins.:33cm long. Circa 1933.

£175 — £250

740. Meccano also produced a scarcer non-constructor sports car, note close resemblance to P type M.G. The model has simple steering mechanism, the exhaust pipe doubles as brake and the windscreen is of perspex with metal frame. Circa 1935.

£200 — £300

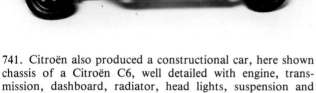

741. Citroën also produced a constructional car, here shown chassis of a Citroën C6, well detailed with engine, transmission, dashboard, radiator, head lights, suspension and bolt-on wheels with Michelin tyres. 15ins.:38cm long. Mid-1930s.

£250 — £350

742. The American firm of Structo, whose slogan was 'Structo toys make men of boys' produced this constructor car, also shown with body removed exposing powerful clockwork motor and simple working gearbox. Circa 1930.

£175 — £250

743. An interesting body style from the 'thirties is shown in these two illustrations of a Günthermann roll-back roof coupé, with electric lights, opening passenger door and trunk. Circa 1930.

£400 — £600

744. The road view of a Marklin constructor (see Colour Plate 37, p. 204) exposing details, rubber tyres, etc.

£300 — £500

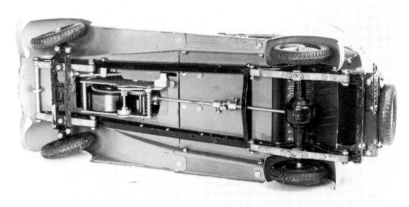

745. Produced by Tipp & Co. and called 'Der Wagen des Führers', this Mercedes tourer is nicely detailed with lamps, horns and twin side-mounted spare wheels (missing in photograph). Finished in dark blue with silver lining. 9ins.:23cm long. Mid- to late 1930s.

£275 — £350

746. Unusual, due to its bakelite construction, this 'Ranlite' Singer saloon with sliding roof and sprung bumpers, was manufactured by Automobiles (Geographical) Ltd. of Halifax, Yorks., and was relatively expensive at 35s. (£1.75) when introduced in 1931.

£150 — £200

747. Produced by Automobiles (Geographical) of Halifax, this Golden Arrow record car is unusual in that it is constructed of bakelite material. Clockwork powered. 17ins.:43cm long. Circa 1935.

£100 — £150

748. Here shown with its original box giving record details, a Tri-ang Magic Midget tinplate and clockwork record car. Finished in green with M.G. Union Jack motif and rubber wheels with polished aluminium discs. 15¾ins.:40cm long. Note photograph and facsimile signature of driver, George Eyston, on box. Circa 1935.

£125 — £175

749. In the mid-'thirties, Tri-ang produced a series of small tinplate and clockwork vehicles, known as Minics, here shown a Ford Y type, £100 saloon. Note the petrol can to running board and white tyres, found only on pre-war models.

£35 — £50

750. Again from the Minic range, a Daimler tourer, this model was produced with such refinements as electric lights and sliding roof (standard tourer shown, pre-war, without extras, fawn with green mudguards). Also shown, a Minic limousine, loosely based on a pre-war Humber.

£40 — £60 Daimler
£20 — £30 Humber

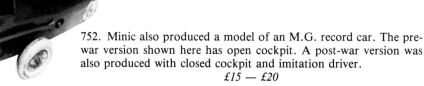

751. Another manufacturer represented by Minic was Vauxhall. Here shown a town sedan, post-war.

£10 — £15

752. Minic also produced a model of an M.G. record car. The pre-war version shown here has open cockpit. A post-war version was also produced with closed cockpit and imitation driver.

£15 — £20

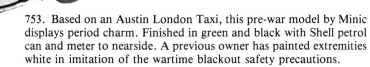

753. Based on an Austin London Taxi, this pre-war model by Minic displays period charm. Finished in green and black with Shell petrol can and meter to nearside. A previous owner has painted extremities white in imitation of the wartime blackout safety precautions.

£20 — £30

754. By Tri-ang Minic, this clockwork Shell and B.P. petrol tanker depicts mechanised man to rear. Note small Shell petrol can on nearside running board indicating pre-war manufacture.

£20 — £30

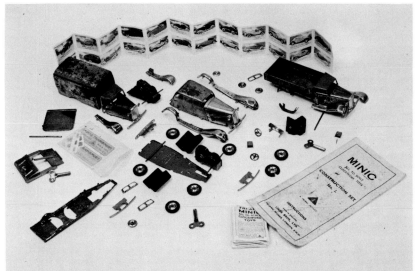

755. Like Meccano, Marklin and others, Minic also produced a construction set. Illustration shows a selection of components from a No. 1 set. Late 1930s.
£50 — £80

756. An attractive and instructive Schuco Mercedes racing car based on W125 and produced pre- and post-war, this toy had detachable wheels with knock-off nuts, detachable steering wheel, working differential, rack and pinion steering, rubber tyres and chrome exhaust. 6ins.:15cm long.
£25 — £40

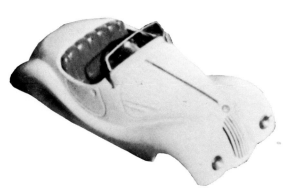

757. By Schuco, this tinplate sports car bears a close resemblance to the BMW 328. It is unusual in having two clockwork motors, one operating a klaxon-like horn, the other for propulsion. Fitted with handbrake and working steering. Produced pre- and post-war (pre-war model shown).
£30 — £50

758. A stylish American tinplate and clockwork G-man pursuit car by Marx, finished in blue and red, very 'thirties.
£50 — £80

759. Using similar pressings to other models from their range, Mettoy produced this tinplate camouflaged staff car in the immediate post-war period. Note close attention to details, numbers, white bumpers, etc. Simple clockwork mechanism. 13¾ins.:35cm long.

£50 — £80

760. Motoring toy interest need not be confined to vehicles. Advertising, especially on Hornby and other model railway items, can form an interesting collection. This 'O' gauge 'Pratts' motor spirit tanker (wheels missing) was produced by the German manufacturer Bing. Circa 1930.

£3 — £4

761. Three pre-war Hornby 'O' gauge petrol and oil tankers, including two varieties of model for Redline-Glico, note die-cast and tinplate filler domes, and a Wakefield Castrol oil tanker. Mid- to late 1930s. Other oil companies covered in this colourful range include Esso, Royal Daylight, Mobiloil and Power.

£7 — £10 each

762. Right, a good example of a 'Power Ethyl' Hornby 'O' gauge petrol tank wagon, shown coupled to a World War II period 'Pool' wagon. During the war petrol companies 'pooled' supplies. Note original utility type box with 'Taxed' stamp. Shown beneath them a scarce 25 series Dinky 'Pool' petrol tanker, circa 1940. Below, a Shell and BP Ethyl motor spirit tanker, c.1940.

£8 — £12 boxed each Hornby
£40 — £60 Dinky

763. America produced 'Tootsie Toy' die-cast cars; illustrated three Buicks with various body styles, late 1920s.
£35 — £50 each

764. An early Dinky product, this high lead content 22 series sports car (No. 22A) was introduced in December 1933, and was not susceptible to the metal fatigue which may be encountered in later 1930s series. Windscreen missing. Finished in scarlet and cream with solid wheels.
£150 — £200

765. Another early Dinky, this No. 22B represents an SS coupé, brightly finished in yellow and green with original plated tinplate radiator surround.
£200 — £300

766. A scarce Britain's two-seater coupé of larger scale but of cruder construction than the Dinkies. These models failed to reach the popularity of their Dinky competitors and three models of civilian cars were produced. Circa 1935.
£40 — £60

767. From across the Atlantic, a 'Tootsie Toy' Graham Paige, die-cast Town sedan with side-mounted spare wheel, finished in blue, tyres showing age cracking. Circa 1935.
£20 — £30

768. Again American, by Manoil, these die-cast models attempt to predict the future styling of motor cars. These unusual models have wooden wheels with rubber tyres. Mid-1930s.
£15 — £30 each

769. Three 'thirties record cars, from left to right, Golden Arrow, Silver Bullet, Bluebird; this time die-cast products by Hill and Co. Bluebird in later form, sizes vary. Silver Bullet 6ins.:15cm long.
£50 — £80 Golden Arrow   *£60 — £100 Silver Bullet*   *£50 — £80 Bluebird*

770. Shortly before World War II, Britain's produced this die-cast model of John Cobb's Napier Railton record car. As in the real car, the body lifts off to expose interesting chassis and engine details.
£250 — £350

771. Small and chunky, this Aero Morgan sports car by Gaiety toys has a plated die-cast body, solid rubber front wheels and is clockwork powered. The sporty feeling has been well captured.

£30 — £50

772. From Dinky's 22 series (No. 229) this streamlined sports car bears a close similarity to the Chrysler Airflow, No. 776, die-cast wheels with rubber tyres, finished in red. Circa 1935.
£50 — £80

773. Dinky's representation of the M.G. car shown here as a set of six racing cars, numbered 23a, various colours, pre-war, shown here with their original box.

£80 — £120

774. Three examples from Dinky's 24 series, left to right: two-seater sports, limousine and sports coupé, all models using Bentley type radiator with badge (just visible). Models from first type 24 series use same radiator without badge. The two-seater sports has a cut-out windscreen and the sports coupé a side-mounted spare wheel. Models have criss-cross chassis. Mid-1930s.

£50 — £80 each

775. From Dinky's 36 series, this scarce Salmson four-seater tourer retains its original driver (very often missing). Mid-1930s.

£50 — £80

776. Produced both pre- and post-war, the Chrysler Airflow started as a 32 series model but shortly after became No. 30A. Finished in various colours, bumpers are fragile and frequently found damaged. Post-war model shown.

£50 — £80

777. From the days when clubs produced their own road warning signs, this Britain's die-cast 'Dangerous Corner' sign bears A.A. motif. 4ins.:10cm high. Circa 1935.

£5 — £10

Colour Plate 41. These C.I.J. P2 Alfa Romeos were produced in the national colours of countries competing in Grand Prix racing, hence silver represents Germany, blue France, red Italy, and green Great Britain. These large size clockwork cars were classic toys from a golden age in motor racing. The silver produced in 1929, the blue 1926. See also nos. 729 and 730, p. 226.

Colour Plate 42. By Lines Bros., this Vauxhall pedal car, circa 1932, conveys the stylish lines of cars of the period. Well constructed, it has a wooden chassis and part body, bonnet of steel with louvres and typical Vauxhall flutes, fold flat windscreen, opening luggage compartment, spare petrol and oil cans, horn and electric lights. Suspension is of leaf spring type with shackles, pneumatic tyres, bumper bars. Available in various colours. This model represents the more expensive and desirable 1930s product. 57ins.:145cm long. See also no. 792, p. 244.

778. As an extension of their extensive range, Dinky produced these figures representing the two major motoring organisations, shown here die-cast figures and motor cycle combinations with tinplate telephone boxes. Introduced 1935.

£25 — £40 set

779. A selection of petrol pumps and oil bins, including a boxed set by Dinky showing 'thirties pump variations. By the 1950s pumps were more streamlined.

£10 — £15 boxed set

780. A selection of pre- and post-war die-cast model road signs produced by Dinky and other manufacturers in various scales. Some signs familiar today, others superseded by more modern representations.

50p each

781. Making its exit from a scarce Dinky tinplate No. 45 garage, a 39 series Buick finished in dark maroon (immediate pre-war).
£25 — £40 garage   £12 — £18 Buick

782. Dinky also produced a London taxi in a variety of colours both pre- and post-war; the model shown is from the immediate post-war period. Note cut-away rear window.
£10 — £15

783. Studebaker land cruiser, an American car of the immediate post-war period, shown here with original box. Dinky, early 1950s.
£8 — £12

784. A set of Dinky sports cars with racing numbers and drivers in overalls, all with original boxes. These cars were also produced without numbers in 'touring' finish, i.e. normally dressed driver. Circa 1955.
£15 — £25 each boxed

785. Far left, a Dinky tanker with 'Regent' transfers, introduced to the range in 1955, shown here with original box. Left, a Dinky Leyland Octopus 'Esso' tanker, introduced in 1958, also shown with original box.
£60 — £80 Regent }
£50 — £70 Esso } *boxed*

786. From the earliest days of the automobile, pedal cars have been produced in imitation of their full-size counterparts. Shown here an Edwardian pedal car of fairly simple construction utilising cycle type transmission and saddle, brass fittings and radially spoked wheels with solid rubber tyres.

£300 — £400

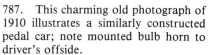

787. This charming old photograph of 1910 illustrates a similarly constructed pedal car; note mounted bulb horn to driver's offside.

788. An unusual two-seater pedal car, possibly constructed from a kit. Wooden chassis, metal bonnet, radiator, adjustable seat. It also has a folding dicky, external hand brake, imitation gear change, wood rimmed steering wheel, and starting handle. Circa 1920.

£300 — £500

ELRCo — **TOY MOTORS** — **ELRCo**

STRONG ATTRACTIVE TOYS.

Body 34 in. Crank drive, fitted with Balloon Discs, Mudguards, Windscreen, Horn, Petrol Can, Mirror and imitation Lamps.
X 1200 2806 - - - - each 39 6
Colour: Powder Blue.

Very well made and finished. Crank Drive. The back axle is sprung on coil springs. Measures 34 in. × 14 in. Fitted with Balloon Discs, Mudguards, Horn, Side Lamps, Petrol Can and Mirror.
X 1202 3906 - - - - each 55 -
Colours: Powder Blue and Red.

Strong Toy, double crank drive. Body 29 in. Seat 12 in. wide. Fitted with 8 × ½ in. Disc Wheels. Rubber tyred. Wired-on tyres.
X 1206 1600 - - - - each 22 6
Painted Red.

Body 38 in., upholstered Seat and Back. Dummy Hood, Horn, Head, Side and Rear Lamps, Licence, Mirror, Petrol Can, Tool Box, Luggage Carrier. Nickel-plated Radiator and Buffer Bar, 1¾ in. Tyres. Aluminium Disc Wheels. **Chain Drive.**
X 1204 8906 - - - - - each £6 5 0
Painted Royal Blue and Fawn, two-colour effect.

Body 42 in. Crank Drive, fitted with Balloon Disc Wheels, Horn and Windscreen.
X 1208 2406 - - - each 35 -
Colours: Powder Blue, or Red.

Chain Drive. Very strongly made Body, measures 36 in. Upholstered Seat and Back. Fitted with Door, N.P. Windscreen, Head and Side Lamps, Petrol Can, Luggage Grid, Clock, Speeds, Dummy Hood, Horn, etc. 16 in. Balloon Disc Wheels.
X 1210 5906 - - - - each 80 -
Colours: Maroon and Grey, two-colour effect.

29-38, GT. EASTERN ST., LONDON, E.C.2.

789. A selection of pedal cars including, lower left, a luxurious model based on Rolls-Royce. Advertised in 1929 East London Rubber Co. autumn catalogue.

790. The leading manufacturer of pedal cars was Lines Bros., who produced a wide range of pedal cars at all prices. Here shown is a more expensive model based on a 1930s Rolls-Royce. Tubular steel chassis with quarter elliptic leaf spring suspension, wooden body with opening steel bonnet, dicky seat, rear-mounted spare wheel, opening door with cast step bearing trademark, and double bumper blades.

£300 — £400

791. Of better proportions than the previous item, this Rolls-Royce, again by Lines Bros., is their much sought-after electric powered version. It is similar in detail to the previous model but has a longer wheelbase chassis with extended bonnet, electric lights, etc. This model was advertised in September 1933 at the then expensive price of 30 guineas and the specification quoted "length 6 feet, height 28½ins., width 28ins., driving unit, 12 volt Lucas powerful electric motor mounted on rear axle; lighting equipment Lucas 5 lamps with 12 volt bulbs (direction indicators are 2 volt only), batteries two 6 volt Lucas car-type; 5 wheels including spare, ballbearing hubs and chromium plated rims, Dunlop 2¼ins. pneumatic tyres, brake, band type operating on rear axle." A magnificent toy.

£800 — £1,200

792. Another Lines Bros. quality product, this Vauxhall pedal car conveys the stylish lines of cars of the period. Wooden chassis and body, steel bonnet, louvred and having typical Vauxhall flutes, plated radiator with real enamelled badge with Vauxhall motif, fold-flat windscreen, opening door to boot, spare petrol and oil cans, electric lights, bulb horn, leaf spring suspension with shackles, pneumatic tyres and spring bumper bars. 57ins.:145cm long. Circa 1932. See also Colour Plate 42, p.239.

£750 — £1,000

793. Based on a Bugatti type 35 racing car, this French-made 'Eureka' model is of entirely pressed steel construction, having treadle drive incorporating free-wheel, well louvred bonnet and body, bolt-on wheels originally produced with electric lights and cycle type mudguards, a side-mounted spare wheel was also carried. Circa 1930. Note this company also produced a Panhard circa 1935. (See page 21, *Catalogue of Model Cars of the World* by Greilsamer and Azema.)

£600 — £900

794. A rather crude 'thirties pedal car of all-metal construction. Opening door, running boards, imitation balloon tyres, bumpers missing, steering wheel damaged. Two models of this car were produced, the 'Chevrolet Regal' and 'Chevrolet Major'. Tri-ang. Circa 1932.

£30 — £50

382

Brown Brothers

TOY MOTORS—*continued*
"RAMBLER" SERIES

Pressed Steel Latest Type Streamline Body, Side Door, Airflow Radiator with Mascot, 9″ Balloon Disc Wheels, ⅞″ Rubber Tyres, Magna Hub Caps, Ball Bearing Back Axle, Front and Rear Pressed Steel Bumpers, Adjustable Windscreen, Number Plate, Head and Side Lamps, Streamline Mudguards, Adjustable Upholstered Seat, Hand Brake, Dummy Hood, Petrol and Oil Cans.
For ages 5 to 7 years. Length 45″. Crank Drive.
No. 27/140cs/4109 .. .. each £3 2 9

Aluminium Streamline Body, Side Door, Latest Type Radiator, 8½″ Tangent-spoked Wheels with Magna Hubs, 1¼″ Jointless Sponge Rubber Tyres, Front and Rear Pressed Steel Bumpers, Adjustable Windscreen, Number Plate, Electric Side Lamps, Dome Steel Mudguards, Dummy Hood, Luggage Locker, Chromium Plated Fittings, Petrol and Oil Cans.
For ages 4 to 6 years. Length 41″. Crank Drive.
No. 27/140e/5208 .. .. each £3 19 0

Pressed Steel Body, Tubular Chassis with Sprung Rear Axle, Side Door, Streamline Radiator, 8½″ Tangent-spoked Wheels, 10″ × 1¼″ Jointless Sponge Rubber Tyres, Magna Hubs, Ball Bearing Back Axle, Front and Rear Tubular Bumpers, Adjustable Windscreen, Number Plate, Dummy Head Lamps, Electric Side Lamps, Stop and Go Sign and Electric Horn, Streamline Mudguards, Adjustable Upholstered Seat, Dummy Hood, Petrol and Oil Cans, Chromium Plated Wheels.
For ages 5 to 7 years Length 45″. Crank and Chain Drive.
No. 27/140g/7506 .. .. each £5 13 3

Pressed Steel, Latest Type Streamline Body, Tubular Chassis, Side Door, Airflow Radiator, 8½″ Tangent-spoked Wheels, 10″ × 1¼″ Jointless Sponge Rubber Tyres, Magna Hubs, Ball Bearing Back Axle, Front and Rear Pressed Steel Bumpers, Adjustable Windscreen, Number Plate, Electric Head Lamps, Stop and Go Sign and Electric Horn, Streamline Mudguards, Adjustable Upholstered Seat, Dummy Hood, Petrol and Oil Cans, Chromium Plated Wheels.
For ages 5 to 7 years. Length 45″. Crank and Chain Drive.
No. 27/140h/7703 .. .. each £5 16 0

Wooden Body, Side Door, Daimler type Radiator with Mascot and Plated Rim, 11″ Tangent-spoked Wheels, 13″ × 1¼″ Jointless Sponge Rubber Tyres, Magna Hubs, Ball Bearing Back Axle. Two sets of Pedals, Front Axle mounted on Springs, Front and Rear Pressed Steel Bumpers, Adjustable Windscreen, Dummy Hood, Head and Side Lamps, Klakker Horn, Hand Brake, Racing Mudguards, Upholstered Seat and Back-rest. Petrol and Oil Cans.
For ages 4 to 8 years. Length 53½″. Crank Drive.
No. 27/140n/6608 .. .. each £5 0 0
Ditto with 12½″ × 2½″ Dunlop Balloon Tyred Wheels, Chromium Plated Fittings.
No. 27/140np 9606 .. .. each £7 4 9

Wooden Body, Tubular Chassis and Sprung Axles, Side Door, Vauxhall Type Radiator, 11″ Tangent-spoked Wheels 13″ × 1¼″ Jointless Sponge Rubber Tyres, Magna Hubs, Ball Bearing Back Axle. Two sets of Pedals, Front and Rear Pressed Steel Bumpers, Adjustable Windscreen, Head and Side Lamps, Racing Mudguards, Upholstered Adjustable Seat and Back-rest, Luggage Locker, Dummy Hood, Petrol and Oil Cans, Nickel Plated Fittings.
For ages 4 to 8 years. Length 52″. Crank Drive.
No. 27/140to/7309 .. .. each £5 11 0
Ditto with 12½″ × 2½″ Dunlop Balloon Tyred Wheels. Chromium Plated Fittings.
No. 27/140tp/10809 .. .. .. each £8 3 3

795. A selection of Lines Bros. Tri-ang pedal cars available through Brown Brothers general catalogue for 1939. Note the specifications and price variations, particularly with regard to tyres, and the typical pre-war necessity for having petrol and oil cans.

£75 — £100 top left   £75 — £100 top right
£100 — £150 centre left   £100 — £150 centre right
£200 — £350 bottom left   £300 — £500 bottom right

796. Note the similarity of this Daimler sports model to the lower left illustration in the Brown Bros. catalogue, with wooden body and chassis, 12½ins. × 2¼ins. pneumatic tyres, coil sprung rear suspension. Tyres for this model are still available, being currently produced for golf trolleys, children's cycles, invalid chairs, etc. 53½ins.:136cm long. Circa 1938.

£200 — £300

797. Another Tri-ang sports car, this Triumph Dolomite has restored wooden body and chassis, pneumatic tyres, rear mounted spare wheel, imitation head lamps, etc. Circa 1938.

£120 — £200

798. The external exhaust pipe with Brooklands fishtail gives some character to this otherwise rather dull post-war pedal racing car of simple pressed steel construction with imitation balloon tyres using thin rubber to periphery of wheel. 47¼ins.:120cm overall. Circa 1946-50.

£50 — £70

799. Produced for only a year or so, this Austin 'Pathfinder Special' was based on the famous supercharged twin cam Austin Seven racing car from the 'thirties. Introduced in 1949 by the Austin pedal car division, the model is of pressed steel (of the same gauge as used on full size cars) and was manufactured by disabled miners in a special factory at Tirybeth, South Wales. Fitted electric horn, detachable bonnet held on by leather straps and pneumatic tyres. 63ins.:160cm long, weight 74½lbs. Also shown, the original catalogue illustration announcing the 'Pathfinder Special'.

£300 — £500

800. From the same factory as the previous model, an example of the well known Austin J40 roadster pedal car produced from 1949 to 1971. The specification included: adjustable treadle drive, handbrake, roller bearing hubs, detachable pressed steel wheels with Dunlop 12½ins. × 2¼ins. tyres, pressed steel bodywork, felt padded seating and leather cloth upholstery, dummy O.H.V. 'engine' complete with sparking plugs and leads, battery operated head lamps and horn, 'chrome trim'. 63ins.:160cm long, 27ins.:69cm wide, 22ins.:56cm high, 43 kilograms. Available in standard Austin colours, approximately 32,000 were produced. Although the model was labelled 'Junior' in catalogues, these models were known as 'Joy cars' by the Austin factory.

£200 — £300

801. A more cheaply made pedal car in the style of a Ford Zephyr, having steering column gear change, bulb horn, bumper bar, windscreen and pressed balloon type wheels and tyres. 39½ins.:100cm long. 1950s.

£40 — £60

Trade Terminology

A light-hearted look at some of the terms used by dealers.

As bought
As purchased — a phrase used to exonerate the vendor of any moral or legal responsibility with regard to the item he is selling (e.g. 'What is it?' 'Not sure, sir, but it's as bought.') Much used by Irish knockers. Auctioneers use similar terms, 'As found' or 'With all faults'.

Bought in
An item unsold at auction, where the price has failed to reach the reserve. Such an item might appear to have been sold, but has failed to reach its reserve and has therefore been 'bought back' by the auctioneer acting on behalf of the vendor.

Collector's piece
Originally a term to describe a fine piece that only a connoisseur would appreciate; often now debased to the sort of thing that only an eccentric enthusiast on the subject would want; normally overpriced, and often totally undesirable.

Commercial
1. Not necessarily a fine or completely original piece, but readily saleable. 2. The description of a dealer's goods as 'commercial' is not a term of approbation and is often used by a specialist or another dealer who is more financially successful.

Estimate
The price suggested by the auctioneer as the amount a lot is likely to fetch. Usually a tortuous compromise between the need to prove to the vendor the auctioneer's competence as a valuer and an effort to persuade as many potential buyers as possible to attend.

Flea market
A collection of stalls where the variety of pieces sold is very considerable, often rubbish, and usually overpriced. Prices asked are normally subject to negotiation.

Fresh
Unseen by dealers in the locality.

Hammer price
The auction price.

Honest
A piece which is 'right', but simple in construction or decoration.

In the book
An attempt to establish an immediate provenance for an item otherwise hard to compliment by reference to standard works, or indeed any printed source. An attempt to confer immediate acceptance and respectability.

Investment item
Used descriptively by a dealer of something for which he has paid too much.

Knocker
One who calls on a private house uninvited and tries to buy goods, usually below current market value.

Knocking down
At auction, the selling of an item.

Knocking out
The selling of goods at very small profit, very quickly, with the object of (a) bringing in money quickly or (b) disposing of an item for which one has paid too much.

Looker
A serious buyer without the funds to acquire any goods.

Old friends
Items of whose company one has tired, which reappear regularly at auction, or those in a shop that have hitherto failed to find a buyer.

Right
An item which proves, on examination, to be of the period which at first sight it seemed to be, and in most important respects is original. Frequently used by antique dealers. (See 'Wrong'.)

Ring
A group of dealers who agree not to increase the price at auction by nominating one of their number to bid. An item so bought is re-auctioned privately afterwards and the difference in value split as agreed between the participants. There may be several opposing rings at one auction. (Illegal under the Auctions (Bidding Agreements) Act 1969.)

Rooms, The
The large auction houses, especially in London. Often used pretentiously in the provinces by those who would like their intimate familiarity with the London auction houses to be assumed.

Runner
One who makes his living by transporting pieces between dealers with a view to making a margin from the prospective sales, usually selling from his vehicle.

Sleeper
A piece which has been untouched for many years and is therefore more desirable than something recently restored.

Speculative
May or may not have considerable value, normally the latter.

Stolen
1. Goods illegally obtained as generally understood. 2. A very cheap purchase (see 'Touch').

Touch
A cheap item with a good profit ('a useful touch': an even better profit might be envisaged).

Trade, The
Antique dealers collectively.

Trade price
Cost of an item to a dealer, usually less than the marked ticket price (e.g. 'What's the trade on...?').

Trotting
1. At auction, the artificial increase in bidding with the intention of raising the selling price (running up). 2. Also used of runners (q.v.) taking their goods from place to place in the hope of finding a buyer.

Unseen
Bought without considered examination, often in the early hours with the aid of a torch.

Wrong
1. Faked, or so heavily adapted from what the item originally was that it now pretends to be what it is not. 2. An out-and-out fake. 3. An item that although possibly desirable has had a considerable amount of restoration, addition or alteration.

Bibliography

(A brief list of more specialised books)

Automobilia — Michael Worthington Williams
Car Mascots — Sirignano & Sulzberger
Motor Badges & Figureheads — Brian Jewell
Catalogue des Verreries de René Lalique
The Art of the Tin Toy — David Pressland
History of the British Dinky Toy — Cecil Gibson
Catalage of Model Cars of the World — J. Greilsamer and B. Azema
Price Guide to Metal Toys — Gardiner & Morris
Collecting Cigarette Cards — Dorothy Bagnell
I.P.M. Catalogue of Picture Postcards — International Postcard Market

In addition, specialised auction catalogues, and original motor
factory catalogues.

The following photographs are courtesy of Sotheby's Belgravia:
Nos. 6, 11, 22, 25, 36, 308, 329, 334, 338, 339, 358, 360-362, 367, 368, 372,
379, 386, 387, 391-395, 397, 398, 416, 418, 423, 564-566, 568, 569, 652, 683,
711, 712, 714, 715, 717, 718, 720-723, 725, 728, 741, 745, 747.

The following photographs are courtesy of Wallis & Wallis, Lewes:
Nos. 2, 21, 30, 43, 60, 61, 88, 90, 91, 92, 98, 100, 107-112, 121, 234, 336, 345,
346, 347, 365, 400, 402, 434, 438.

Index

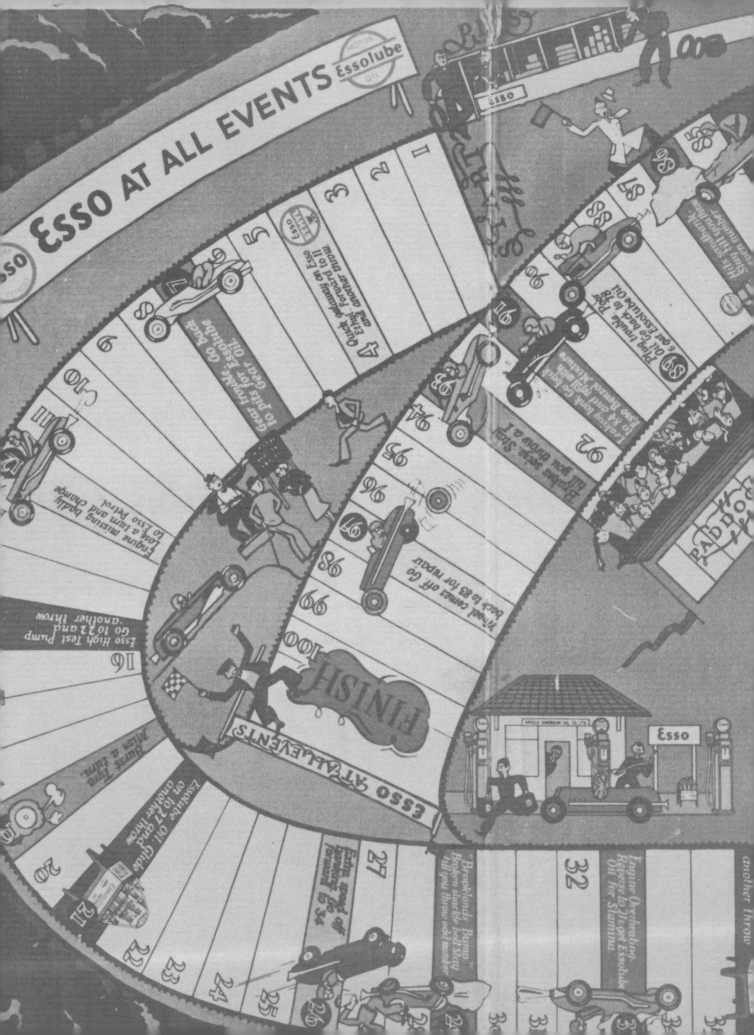